CANADIAN SOCCER'S ALL-TIME
Top 100
MEN'S FOOTBALLERS

• • •

CANADIAN SOCCER'S
TOP 100 MEN'S FOOTBALLERS
(1973 - 2023)

footballMedia / by Richard Scott
Copyright © 2023-2024 Up North Productions.
No reproduction without permission.
All rights reserved. April 2024.
ISBN 978-1-7383469-2-9

Published in Canada by:
Up North Productions
1995 Indian Creek Road
Limoges, ON   K0A 2M0
books@footballmedia.ca

*Cover design by Griffin Scott. Cyle Larin cover photo by Richard Scott.
All headshots courtesy and credit Canada Soccer.*

CANADIAN SOCCER'S TOP 100 MEN'S FOOTBALLERS (1973 - 2023)

CANADA'S ULTIMATE SQUAD	6
CANADA SOCCER HALL OF FAME	7
CANADIAN SOCCER'S TOP 100 MEN'S FOOTBALLERS FROM 1973 - 2023	8
MORE TOP FOOTBALLERS FROM THE 1940s - 1970s	108

● ● ●

CANADIAN SOCCER'S TOP 100

PAGE	TOP 100 FOOTBALLERS		JERSEY & POSITION		CANADA "A"		MP	/ G
8	Adekugbe, Sam		3	LB / LW	2013	2023	42	1g
9	Arfield, Scott		8	M	2016	2020	19	2g
10	Aunger, Geoff		14	M	1990	1997	44	4g
11	Ayre, Garry	H.O.F.	2	M / CB	1973	1977	16	
12	Bent, Jason		6	M	1996	2003	32	
13	Bernier, Patrice	H.O.F.	8	M	2003	2017	56	2g
14	Biello, Mauro		20	M	1995	2004	4	
15	Bolitho, Bob	H.O.F.	10	RB / DM	1974	1981	22	2g
16	Borjan, Milan		18	GK	2011	2023	80	
17	Brand, Jack	H.O.F.	1	GK	1974	1977	0	
18	Brennan, Jim	H.O.F.	11	LB / LM	1999	2008	49	6g
19	Bridge, Ian	H.O.F.	6	CB	1981	1991	35	5g
20	Buchanan, Tajon		11	W	2021	2023	35	4g
21	Bunbury, Alex	H.O.F.	9	F	1986	1999	65	15g
22	Catliff, John	H.O.F.	10	F	1984	1994	45	18g
23	Cavallini, Lucas		9	F	2012	2023	40	19g
24	Chursky, Tony	H.O.F.	1	GK	1972	1981	20	
25	Corazzin, Carlo	H.O.F.	9	F	1992	2004	59	11g
26	Crépeau, Maxime		16	GK	2014	2023	15	
27	Dasović, Nick	H.O.F.	8	M	1992	2004	63	2g
28	David, Jonathan		20	F	2018	2023	45	26g
29	Davies, Alphonso		19	FB / W	2017	2023	44	15g
30	de Guzman, Julian		6	M	2002	2016	89	4g
31	de Jong, Marcel		17	LB	2007	2018	56	3g
32	De Rosario, Dwayne	H.O.F.	14	F / AM	1996	2015	81	22g
33	deVos, Jason	H.O.F.	5	CB	1996	2004	49	4g
34	Dolan, Paul	H.O.F.	1	GK	1984	1997	53	
35	Douglas, Jimmy	H.O.F.	6	M	1972	1976	15	1g
36	Dunfield, Terry		7	M	2004	2013	14	1g
37	Edgar, David		5	CB / FB	2007	2019	42	4g
38	Eustáquio, Stephen		7	M	2019	2023	34	4g
39	Fenwick, Paul		2	CB	1993	2003	33	
40	Fletcher, Carl		13	CB	1991	2003	40	2g
41	Forrest, Craig	H.O.F.	1	GK	1988	2001	56	
42	Friend, Rob		9	F	2003	2012	32	2g
43	Gerba, Ali		10	F	2005	2011	31	15g
44	Gray, Gerry	H.O.F.	8	M	1980	1991	35	2g
45	Hainault, André		4	CB	2006	2016	44	2g
46	Hastings, Richard	H.O.F.	3	LB / CB	1998	2010	59	1g
47	Henry, Doneil		15	CB	2012	2022	44	1g
48	Hirschfeld, Lars		1	GK	1999	2015	48	
49	Hoilett, Junior		10	W	2015	2023	62	16g
50	Hooper, Lyndon	H.O.F.	8	M	1986	1997	67	1g
51	Hume, Iain		7	F	2003	2016	43	6g
52	Hutchinson, Atiba		13	M	2002	2023	104	9g
53	Iarusci, Robert	H.O.F.	2	RB / CB	1976	1983	27	2g
54	Imhof, Daniel		8	M	2000	2010	36	
55	Jackson, Simeon		10	F	2008	2017	49	6g
56	Jaković, Dejan		4	CB	2008	2020	41	1g
57	Jazić, Ante		3	FB	1998	2012	35	1g

4 | Canadian Soccer

MEN'S FOOTBALLERS (1973-2023)

PAGE	TOP 100 FOOTBALLERS	H.O.F.	Jersey	Position	\multicolumn{2}{c}{CANADA "A"}	MP	G
58	Johnson, Glen	H.O.F.	8	F	1972	1976	8	1g
59	Johnson, Will		8	M	2005	2019	45	4g
60	Johnston, Alistair		2	FB	2021	2023	39	1g
61	Kaye, Mark-Anthony		14	M	2017	2023	42	2g
62	Klukowski, Mike		3	FB	2003	2012	36	
63	Kodelja, Victor	H.O.F.	7	F / FB	1974	1977	8	
64	Larin, Cyle		17	F	2014	2023	65	28g
65	Laryea, Richie		22	FB	2019	2023	48	1g
66	Ledgerwood, Nik		6	M / FB	2007	2017	50	1g
67	Lenarduzzi, Bob	H.O.F.	5	FB / M	1972	1986	48	5g
68	Lenarduzzi, Sam	H.O.F.	6	FB / CB	1968	1981	29	
69	Lettieri, Tino	H.O.F.	1	GK	1975	1988	24	
70	Limniatis, John	H.O.F.	8	CB / M	1987	1997	45	1g
71	Marcantonio, Carmine	H.O.F.	18	M / CB	1976	1981	2	
72	McGrane, John	H.O.F.	17	CB / F	1976	1983	13	
73	McKenna, Kevin	H.O.F.	4	CB / F	2000	2012	63	11g
74	McLeod, Wes	H.O.F.	8	LM	1975	1985	18	1g
75	Miller, Colin	H.O.F.	6	M	1983	1997	61	5g
76	Miller, Kamal		4	CB / FB	2019	2023	41	
77	Mitchell, Dale	H.O.F.	14	F	1977	1993	55	19g
78	Mobilio, Domenic	H.O.F.	14	F	1986	1997	25	3g
79	Moore, Terry	H.O.F.	4	CB	1981	1986	12	
80	Nakajima-Farran, Issey		11	W / F	2006	2016	38	1g
81	Nash, Martin		7	M	1997	2008	38	2g
82	Occean, Olivier		17	F	2004	2012	28	6g
83	Onstad, Pat	H.O.F.	18	GK	1988	2010	59	
84	Osorio, Jonathan		21	M	2013	2023	71	9g
85	Pakos, George		13	M / F	1983	1986	23	5g
86	Parsons, Les (Buzz)	H.O.F.	9	F	1972	1980	24	7g
87	Peschisolido, Paul	H.O.F.	10	F / RM	1992	2004	53	10g
88	Piette, Samuel		6	M	2012	2023	67	
89	Radzinski, Tomasz	H.O.F.	9	F / LW	1994	2009	46	10g
90	Ragan, Randy	H.O.F.	4	M	1980	1986	38	
91	Ricketts, Tosaint		11	M / F	2009	2020	61	17g
92	Robinson, Brian	H.O.F.	4	M / CB	1972	1977	16	1g
93	Samuel, Randy	H.O.F.	5	CB / FB	1983	1997	82	
94	Šegota, Branko	H.O.F.	20	F	1980	1988	20	3g
95	Simpson, Josh		11	LW	2004	2012	43	4g
96	Stalteri, Paul	H.O.F.	7	RB / RM	1996	2011	84	7g
97	Stamatopoulos, Kenny		13	GK	2001	2016	21	
98	Stojanović, Mike		7	F	1980	1981	15	5g
99	Straith, Adam		15	CB / DM	2010	2019	43	
100	Sutton, Greg		1	GK	1999	2009	16	
101	Sweeney, Mike		11	M / FB	1980	1993	61	1g
102	Valentine, Carl	H.O.F.	7	F / W	1985	1993	31	1g
103	Vitória, Steven		5	CB	2016	2023	46	5g
104	Watson, Mark	H.O.F.	3	CB	1991	2005	78	3g
105	Wilson, Bruce	H.O.F.	3	FB	1971	1986	57	
106	Wotherspoon, David		8	M	2018	2023	13	1g
107	Yallop, Frank	H.O.F.	2	FB / CB	1990	1997	52	

CANADA'S ULTIMATE SQUAD

GOALKEEPER
1 • CRAIG FORREST
Canada's number one goalkeeper at the 2001 FIFA Confederations Cup and MVP of the 2000 Concacaf Gold Cup.

GOALKEEPER
18 • MILAN BORJAN
Canada's number one goalkeeper at the 2022 FIFA World Cup and Canada's all-time leader in clean sheets.

RIGHT BACK / M
7 • PAUL STALTERI
Career 225 appearances across the Bundesliga and Premier League. Was most often at right back or midfield.

LEFT BACK
3 • BRUCE WILSON
Captain at the 1984 Olympic Games and 1986 FIFA World Cup. Named to the Concacaf Team of the Century.

CENTRE BACK
5 • RANDY SAMUEL
Played every minute for Canada at the 1986 FIFA World Cup. Played in the first division in Netherlands.

MIDFIELDER
13 • ATIBA HUTCHINSON
Canada's captain at the 2022 FIFA World Cup. In Europe featured in 16 seasons of UEFA club competitions.

MIDFIELDER
6 • JULIAN DE GUZMAN
Career 175 appearances across the Bundesliga and La Liga. MVP at the 2007 Concacaf Gold Cup.

RIGHT WING / AM
10 • JUNIOR HOILETT
Career 161 appearances in the Premier League. Former Canada record holder for Men's National Team assists.

ATTACKING MID / F
14 • DALE MITCHELL
Canada's top goalscorer at the 1984 Olympic Games. Played forward as well as midfield for Canada.

LEFT WING / LB
19 • ALPHONSO DAVIES
UEFA Champions League winner. Scored Canada's first goal at men's FIFA World Cup.

FORWARD
20 • JONATHAN DAVID
Canada record holder for most goals in a Top-5 European league. Already 25 goals with Canada in 45 matches.26

FORWARD
9 • TOMASZ RADZINSKI
Top scorer in Belgium before he scored 35 Premier League goals in 193 career appearances.

RIGHT BACK / CB
2 • ROBERT IARUSCI
Four-time NASL Championship winner. Captain when Canada came within a goal of the 1982 FIFA World Cup.

CENTRE BACK
5 • JASON DEVOS
Winning captain at the 2000 Concacaf Gold Cup. Also played every minute at 2001 FIFA Confederations Cup.

CENTRE BACK / FB
3 • SAM LENARDUZZI
Held Canada record for international appearances. Helped Canada finish fourth in Concacaf in 1977.

ATTACKING MID / F
14 • DWAYNE DE ROSARIO
More than 100 MLS goals and four-time MLS Cup winner. Once had Canada record for Men's National Team "A" goals.

FORWARD
9 • ALEX BUNBURY
Once held Canada record for goals in FIFA World Cup Qualifiers. Notably played in England and Portugal.

FORWARD
17 • CYLE LARIN
Canada's all-time record holder for Men's National Team goals. Top scorer in 2021-22 Concacaf Final Round.

CANADA SOCCER HALL OF FAME

The Canada Soccer Hall of Fame honours greats of the game from more than 150 years of football in Canada. From 2000 to 2024, the Canada Soccer Hall of Fame has honoured its first 212 members who were either players, coaches/managers, referees or builders.

MODERN (MNT)
Patrice Bernier
Jim Brennan
Ian Bridge
Alex Bunbury
John Catliff
Carlo Corazzin
Nick Dasovic
Dwayne De Rosario
Jason deVos
Paul Dolan
Craig Forrest
Gerry Gray
Richard Hastings
Lyndon Hooper
John Limniatis
Kevin McKenna
Colin Miller
Dale Mitchell
• Domenic Mobilio
Terry Moore
Pat Onstad
Paul Peschisolido
Tomasz Radzinski
Randy Ragan
Randy Samuel
Branko Segota
Paul Stalteri
Mike Sweeney
Carl Valentine
Mark Watson
Frank Yallop

MODERN (WNT)
Sue Brand
Silvana Burtini Gerela
Connie Cant
Annie Caron
Candace Chapman
Carla Chin Baker
Tracy David
Geri Donnelly
Martina Franko
Robyn Gayle
Randee Hermus

Charmaine Hooper
Angela Kelly
Kara Lang
Karina LeBlanc
Janet Lemieux
Joan McEachern
Luce Mongrain
Isabelle Morneau
Carmelina Moscato
Suzanne Muir
Andrea Neil
Michelle Ring Passant
Cathy Ross
Carrie Serwetnyk
Sue Simon
Helen Stoumbos
Brittany Timko Baxter
Amy Walsh
Rhian Wilkinson
Janine Wood Helland

PAST (POST WW2)
• Frank Ambler
• Dick Arends
Garry Ayre
• Eddie Bak
• Jim Blundell
Bob Bolitho
Jack Brand
• Roy Cairns
• Marcel Castonguay
• Paul Castonguay
• Roland Castonguay
Tony Chursky
• Jack Cowan
• Errol Crossan
Jimmy Douglas
Neil Ellett
• Bill Gill
• Doug Greig
• Trevor Harvey
• Art Hughes
Robert Iarusci
• Gordon Ion
Glen Johnson

Victor Kodelja
Bob Lenarduzzi
Sam Lenarduzzi
Tino Lettieri
Carmine Marcantonio
• Don Matheson
John McGrane
Normie McLeod
Wes McLeod
• Doug McMahon
• Bobby Newbold
Les Buzz Parsons
• Ken Pears
• Brian Philley
• Pat Philley
• Harry Phillips
Brian Robinson
John Schepers
Bobby Smith
• Jimmy Spencer
• Andy Stevens
Gary Stevens
• Gogie Stewart
• Mike Stojanović
David Stothard
Gene Vazzoler
• Jackie Whent
• Fred Whittaker
Bruce Wilson
• NIR/Jimmy Nicholl

PAST (PRE WW2)
• George Anderson
• Walter Bowman
• Geordie Campbell
• Joe Clulow
• Jock Coulter
• Eddie Derby
• Fred Dierden
• Ernie Edmunds
• Bill Findler
• Pete Larry Fitzpatrick
• George Graham
• Art Halliwell
• Bob Harley

• Bobby Lavery
• Eddie MacLaine
• Harry Manson
• Bill Matthews
• Jimmy Moir
• Jimmy Nelson
• Alec Smith
• Dickie Stobbart
• Tiny Thombs
• Dr. Walter Thomson
• Dave Turner
• Stan Wakelyn
• Artie Woutersz
• ENG/Sam Chedgzoy
• SCO/Joe Kennaway
• NIR/Whitey McDonald

BUILDER
• George Anderson
• Arthur Arnold
Brian Avey
Angus Barrett
• Herb Capozzi
• Jeff Cross
• Sam Davidson
• Sam Donaghey
• Gus Etchegarry
• Billy Fenton
• Jim Fleming
• David Forsyth
• Dr. Tom Fried
• Dave Fryatt
Bill Gilhespy
• Dr. Rudy Gittens
• George Gross
• Bill Hoyle
• Jim Hubay
• Alex Hylan
Colin Jose
• Johnny Kerr
• Eric King
• Graham Leggat
• John McMahon
• Lou Moro
Kevin Muldoon

Christine O'Connor
• Len Peto
Pat Quinn
• Terry Quinn
• John Richardson
• Tom Robertson
• John Russell
• Aubrey Sanford
Bob Sayer
Georges Schwartz
• Bill Simpson
Leeta Sokalski
• Alan Southard
• Dr. Fred Stambrook
• Steve Stavro
• Bill Stirling
Les Wilson
• Derek Wisdom

COACH-MANAGER
• Jimmie Adam
• Bob Bearpark
Sylvie Béliveau
Chris Bennett
Stuart Brown
• John Buchanan
Bert Goldberger
Dick Howard
• Don Petrie
• Ted Slade
• Bill Thomson
Bruce Twamley
• Tony Waiters

REFEREE
Gord Arrowsmith
Sonia Denoncourt
Tony Evangelista
• Dan Kulai
• Horace Lyons
• Ray Morgan
Bob Sawtell
• Dino Soupliotis
Héctor Vergara
Werner Winsemann

LEFT BACK / LW

SAM ADEKUGBE

Born: 1995-01-16, London, ENG. Grew up in Calgary, AB, CAN. Height 178 cm. Dominant left foot.

1 FIFA World Cup: Group phase at Qatar 2022
1 Concacaf medal: Silver in 2022-23 CNL
1st #CANMNT: 2015-09-08 at Belmopán, BLZ (v. BLZ)
1st Goal: 2022-01-30 at Hamilton, ON, CAN (v. USA)

CANADA HIGHLIGHTS

Sam Adekugbe represented Canada at the FIFA World Cup Qatar 2022 after helping his nation finish first in the 2021-22 Concacaf Final Round of FIFA World Cup Qualifiers. He then won a Concacaf Silver Medal at the 2022-23 Nations League Finals in Las Vegas.

Adekugbe has already represented Canada in two cycles of FIFA World Cup Qualifiers and one edition of the Concacaf Gold Cup. In 2021-22 FIFA World Cup Qualifiers, he scored his first international "A" goal in a 2-0 home win over USA at Tim Hortons Field in Hamilton.

At the FIFA World Cup in Qatar, his shot from the left side in the group finale was deflected for a Morocco own goal.

VANCOUVER WHITECAPS FC

Adekugbe rejoined Vancouver Whitecaps FC in August 2023 after seven seasons in Europe. He played in England, Sweden, Norway and Turkey and left Europe as a 2022-23 Turkish Süper Lig winner with Galatasaray SK. He had played at Hatayspor FC before a deadly earthquake ended their 2022-23 season.

Adekugbe played his youth soccer in England and Canada. He helped Whitecaps FC win the Canadian Championship in 2015.

CANADA RECORDS

"A" RECORDS	MP	MS	MIN	G	A
2013 CANADA	0	0	0		
2014 CANADA	0	0	0		
2015 CANADA	2	0	44		
2016 CANADA	1	0	12		
2017 CANADA	3	2	189		
2018 CANADA	1	0	31		
2019 CANADA	2	1	110		
2020 CANADA	2	2	169		
2021 CANADA	13	6	655		2a
2022 CANADA	13	10	870	1g	2a
2023 CANADA	5	2	234		
UNTIL DEC.2023	42	23	2314	1g	4a
FWC QUALIFIERS	19	11	1112	1g	2a
GOLD CUP	2	2	180		
NATIONS LEAGUE	8	4	445		1a

FIFA WORLD CUP	MP	MS	MIN		
2022 FIFA WC	3	1	94		

● ● ●

2022 FIFA WORLD CUP • Sam Adekugbe featured in all three Canada matches at the FIFA World Cup in Qatar. Across three matches, he delivered five crosses and completed 93.8% of his passes. In his start against Morocco, he got around Achraf Hakimi down the left side and fired a low shot that Nayaf Aguerd redirected into his own goal.

8

SCOTT ARFIELD

MIDFIELDER

Born: 1988-11-01, Livingston, SCO. Height 178 cm.
Dominant right foot.

1 cycle FIFA World Cup Qualifiers: 2016
1st #CANMNT: 2016-03-25 at Vancouver, BC, CAN (v. MEX)
1st Goal: 2017-07-07 at Harrison, NJ, USA (v. GUF)

CANADA HIGHLIGHTS

Scott Arfield has made 17 international "A" appearances, including five starts wearing the captain's armband. He has represented Canada in one cycle of FIFA World Cup Qualifiers, two editions of the Concacaf Gold Cup, and one edition of Concacaf Nations League. He was Canada's runner up in Player of the Year voting in 2017.

Arfield was 27 years old when he made his Canada debut against Mexico on 25 March 2016 in front of a Canadian record crowd at Vancouver's BC Place. In 2019, he captained Canada to a 2-0 win over USA in Concacaf Nations League, Canada's first win over the Americans in 34 years.

CHARLOTTE FC

Arfield joined Charlotte FC in June 2023 after 16 seasons in Scotland's Premiership, England's Championship and the Premier League. He helped Burnley FC earn promotion from the Championship as league runners up in 2013-14 and league winners in 2015-16. He played three seasons in the Premier League.

In Scotland, he played five seasons at Rangers FC where they won the Premiership in 2020-21. They won the Scottish Cup in 2022 and reached the last 16 in UEFA Europa League in 2019-20.

Before moving to England, Arfield got his start in Scotland with Falkirk FC. He was just 18 years old when he made his Scottish Premiership debut on 4 August 2007. He moved to Huddersfield Town FC and helped the club win a playoff promotion from League One to the Championship in 2012.

CANADA RECORDS

"A" RECORDS	MP	MS	MIN	G	A
2016 CANADA	6	5	495		3a
2017 CANADA	6	6	539	1g	1a
2018 CANADA	1	1	90		1a
2019 CANADA	6	5	480	1g	2a
2020 CANADA	0	0	0		
5 SEASONS	**19**	**17**	**1604**	**2g**	**7a**
FWC QUALIFIERS	3	2	315		1a
GOLD CUP	8	7	660	2g	2a
NATIONS LEAGUE	2	2	180		1a

1st INTERNATIONAL GOAL • Scott Arfield scored his first international goal in a 4-2 win over French Guiana in his Concacaf Gold Cup debut in 2017. He scored on his own rebound late in the first half. Four days later, he set up Alphonso Davies for the opening goal in a 1-1 draw with Costa Rica.

MIDFIELDER

GEOFF AUNGER

14

Born: 1968-02-04, Red Deer, AB, CAN. Grew up in Coquitlam, BC, CAN. Height 180 cm. Dominant right foot.

2 cycles FIFA World Cup Qualifiers: 1992-93, 1996-97
1st #CANMNT: 1991-03-14 at Los Angeles, CA, USA (v. MEX B)
1st Goal: 1992-11-15 at Burnaby, BC, CAN (v. BER)

CANADA HIGHLIGHTS

Geoff Aunger made 44 international "A" appearances for Canada from 1990 to 1997, including two cycles of FIFA World Cup Qualifiers. He helped Canada reach FIFA's intercontinental playoff in 1993 and the Concacaf Final Round in 1997. He featured in Canada's historic 1-1 draw in 1994 with Brazil in front of a Canadian record crowd at Edmonton's Commonwealth Stadium.

He was 23 years old when he made his Canada debut at the 1991 Three Nations Cup and he was 24 when he made his international "A" debut a year later in a 5-2 win over China PR at Victoria's Royal Athletic Park. He scored his first goal in 1992 FIFA World Cup Qualifiers against Bermuda at Burnaby's Swangard Stadium, then scored the opening goal of a 2-2 draw with Martinique at the 1993 Concacaf Gold Cup at the famous Estadio Azteca.

CLUB HIGHLIGHTS

Aunger played his club football in Canada, England and the United States, notably winning both the MLS Supporters' Shield and MLS Cup in 1999 with D.C. United. He also played in the 1998 MLS All-Star Game.

Aunger played six seasons in the Canadian Soccer League with the Vancouver 86ers, Winnipeg Fury, Victoria Vistas, Hamilton Steelers and London Lasers. He was named to the CSL All-Star Team in 1992. He then helped the 86ers win the APSL regular-season title in 1993.

CANADA RECORDS

"A" RECORDS	MP	MS	MIN	G	A
1990 CANADA	0	0	0		
1991 CANADA	0	0	0		
1992 CANADA	6	2	-	1g	1a
1993 CANADA	6	4	355	1g	1a
1994 CANADA	5	3	300		
1995 CANADA	9	8	713	1g	2a
1996 CANADA	8	8	606	1g	3a
1997 CANADA	10	8	690		
8 SEASONS	**44**	**33**	**n/a**	**4g**	**7a**
FWC QUALIFIERS	17	14	1117	2g	1a
GOLD CUP	5	4	329	1g	3a
3 NATIONS CUP	1	0	16		

● ● ●

FIFA WORLD CUP QUALIFIERS • Geoff Aunger helped Canada reach the Concacaf Final Round in back-to-back cycles of FIFA World Cup Qualifiers in 1992-93 and 1996-97. In 1996 at Edmonton, he scored from the penalty spot in a 3-1 win over Panama and got an assist in the 2-0 win over Cuba.

2

GARRY AYRE

MIDFIELDER / CB

Born: 1953-10-12, Vancouver, BC, CAN. Height 180 cm.

1 Olympic Games: Group phase at Montréal 1976
1 cycle FIFA World Cup Qualifiers: 1976-77
1st #CANMNT: 1973-09-28 at Valletta, MLT (v. MLT)

 CANADA SOCCER HALL OF FAME

Garry Ayre made 34 international appearances for Canada, ranked third all-time after his last Canada match on 22 October 1977 in Monterrey, Mexico. Across five years, he played at the 1975 Pan American Games in Mexico, Canada's home Olympic Games at Montréal 1976, and the 1976-77 FIFA World Cup Qualifiers. In the 1977 Concacaf Final Round, Canada finished fourth in the region.

Ayre was just 19 years old when he made his Canada debut on 28 September 1973 in Valletta, Malta. He played two matches at the 1975 Pan American Games, including the "Puebla punch up" when he was ejected for retaliation and before Canada eventually pulled out of the tournament.

In 1977, Ayre led Canada in minutes played as he featured in every minute across six international matches.

At the club level, Ayre was an NASL Championship winner with the 1978 New York Cosmos. He played four seasons in the NASL between the Vancouver Whitecaps, Cosmos and Portland Timbers from 1977 to 1980.

Before turning pro, he played in the old Pacific Coast League where he scored his first goal at age 18 as a junior call up with the Vancouver Firefighters in 1971-72. He also played in the BC Premier League and BC League. In 1973, he helped the British Columbia U-21 side win a Gold Medal at the Canada Games.

CANADA RECORDS

INT'L RECORDS	MP	MS	MIN
1973 CANADA	6	6	540
1974 CANADA	5	1	178
1975 CANADA	10	10	-
1976 CANADA	7	7	-
1977 CANADA	6	6	540
5 SEASONS	**34**	**30**	**n/a**
FWC QUALIFIERS	7	7	630

OLYMPIC GAMES	MP	MS	MIN
1976 OLYMPIC	2	2	180

1976 OLYMPIC GAMES • Fullback Garry Ayre played in every Canada minute at the 1976 Olympic Football Tournament with matches played in Montréal and Toronto. His free kick in the 3-1 loss to Korea DPR led to Canada's lone goal at Varsity Stadium (scored by Jimmy Douglas in the 51st minute).

DEFENSIVE MID / RB

JASON BENT

Born: 1977-03-08, Scarborough, ON, CAN. Grew up in Brampton, ON, CAN. Height 175 cm. Dominant right foot.

1 FIFA Confederations Cup: Group phase in 2001
2 cycles FIFA World Cup Qualifiers: 1997, 2000
1st #CANMNT: 1997-10-12 at Edmonton, AB, CAN (v. MEX)

CANADA HIGHLIGHTS

Jason Bent made 32 career international "A" appearances for Canada across eight years from 1996 to 2003, including the 2001 FIFA Confederations Cup in Japan.

Bent was part of the squad that helped Canada qualify for the 2000 Concacaf Gold Cup, but he missed the final tournament through a knee injury. He came back healthy that summer and was one of two players that featured in every Canada minute across FIFA World Cup Qualifiers in 2000.

He was 20 years old when he made his international "A" debut on 12 October 1997 against Mexico in the Concacaf Final Round of FIFA World Cup Qualifiers. He helped Canada set a program record with a 15-match undefeated streak in 1999-2000 and he helped Canada finish in third place at the 2002 Concacaf Gold Cup.

Bent won the 1996 Concacaf Youth Championship and represented Canada at both the FIFA U-17 World Cup in 1993 and the FIFA U-20 World Cup in 1997.

CLUB HIGHLIGHTS

Bent helped Plymouth Argyle FC win promotion twice in three years, winning the English Third Division in 2001-02 and the Second Division in 2003-04.

In 1997-98, he was just 20 years old when he made his pro debut with FSV Zwickau in the 2.Bundesliga. In Major League Soccer, he helped the Colorado Rapids reach the US Open Cup Final in 1999.

CANADA RECORDS

"A" RECORDS	MP	MS	MIN
1996 CANADA	0	0	0
1997 CANADA	3	3	225
1998 CANADA	1	1	90
1999 CANADA	6	5	495
2000 CANADA	12	11	940
2001 CANADA	4	4	360
2002 CANADA	3	2	167
2003 CANADA	3	3	249
8 SEASONS	**32**	**29**	**2526**
GOLD CUP	4	3	236

CONFEDERATIONS	MP	MS	MIN
2001 FIFA CC	3	3	270

2001 FIFA CONFEDERATIONS CUP • Jason Bent featured in every Canada minute at the FIFA Confederations Cup in Japan in 2001. After a 3-0 loss to the hosts in the opener, Bent helped Canada post a 0-0 draw against Brazil, who were just a year away from winning the 2002 FIFA World Cup.

8

PATRICE BERNIER

MIDFIELDER

Born: 1979-09-23, Brossard, QC, CAN. Height 177 cm. Dominant right foot.

3 cycles FIFA World Cup Qualifiers: 2004, 2008, 2011-12
1st #CANMNT: 2003-11-15 at Teplice, CZE (v. CZE)
1st Goal: 2009-06-30 at Oxnard, CA, USA (v. GUA)

 CANADA SOCCER HALL OF FAME

Patrice Bernier made 56 international "A" appearances across 15 years with Canada from 2003 to 2017, including three cycles of FIFA World Cup Qualifiers and four editions of the Concacaf Gold Cup. He helped Canada reach the Concacaf Semifinals in 2007 and the Quarterfinals in both 2009 and 2017.

After representing Canada at the FIFA U-17 World Cup Ecuador 1995, the Pan American Games Winnipeg 1999, and the 2001 Jeux de la Francophonie, Bernier made his international "A" debut on 15 November 2003 against the Czech Republic.

At the club level, he was a Concacaf Champions League finalist and two-time Canadian Championship winner with the Impact de Montréal. He was the team's Most Valuable Player in 2012 and he led all Canadians in MLS minutes played in 2013. In retirement, he was inducted to the club's Wall of Fame.

In Europe, Bernier played in Norway, Germany and Denmark. With FC Nordsjælland, he was a two-time Danish Cup winner.

An eight-time Soccer Québec professional player of the year, he was inducted to the Soccer Québec Hall of Fame at the time of his retirement.

CANADA RECORDS

"A" RECORDS		MP	MS	MIN	G	A
2003	CANADA	2	1	106		
2004	CANADA	4	3	281		
2005	CANADA	8	6	564		
2006	CANADA	5	4	356		1a
2007	CANADA	9	7	641		1a
2008	CANADA	9	5	412		2a
2009	CANADA	6	5	498	2g	
2010	CANADA	2	2	180		
2011	CANADA	1	1	81		
2012	CANADA	3	2	159		
2014	CANADA	2	2	107		1a
2015	CANADA	2	0	63		
2017	CANADA	3	3	210		
15 SEASONS		**56**	**41**	**3658**	**2**	**5a**
FWC QUALIFIERS		12	8	683		1a
GOLD CUP		14	13	1127	1g	1a

1st INTERNATIONAL GOAL • Patrice Bernier played in every Canada match at three straight Concacaf Gold Cups from 2005 to 2009. He scored his first international goal just ahead of the 2009 tournament in a friendly against Guatemala. Less than two weeks later, he scored his second goal in a 2-2 draw with Costa Rica at the 2009 Concacaf Gold Cup.

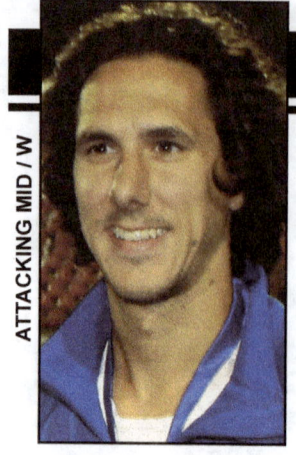

ATTACKING MID / W

20
MAURO BIELLO

Born: 1972-08-08, Montréal, QC, CAN. Height 175 cm. Dominant right foot.

2 cycles FIFA World Cup Qualifiers: 1997, 2004
1st #CANMNT: 1995-10-11 at Concepción, CHI (v. CHI)

CANADA HIGHLIGHTS

Mauro Biello represented Canada in two cycles of FIFA World Cup Qualifiers and helped Canada qualify for the 2000 Concacaf Gold Cup. He was 23 years old when he made his international "A" debut on 11 October 1995 against Chile at Concepción. As a youth international, he represented Canada at the FIFA U-16 World Tournament Scotland 1989.

CLUB HIGHLIGHTS

Biello was a club legend at the Impact de Montréal where he won both the APSL Championship in 1994 and the USL First Division Championship in 2004 and 2009, five Commissioner's Cups as regular season champions from 1995 to 2006, and the Voyageurs Cup as a Canadian Championship winner in 2008. He was a four-time club MVP and two-time league all-star. He retired as the club's all-time leader in appearances, minutes played, goals and assists. He wore the captain's armband from 2002 to 2009 and was inducted to the team's Wall of Fame in 2022.

Biello was also a double winner in one season with the Rochester Raging Rhinos in 1999, capturing the US Open Championship as well as the USL First Division regular season's Commissioner's Cup. Alongside his outdoor career, he played indoor soccer for the Impact, Buffalo Blizzard and Toronto NightHawks.

Before joining the Impact, Biello played two seasons in the Canadian Soccer League with FC Supra Montréal. He was just 18 years old when he made his professional debut on 26 July 1991.

CANADA RECORDS

"A" RECORDS	MP	MS	MIN
1995 CANADA	1	0	45
1997 CANADA	1	1	45
1999 CANADA	1	0	9
2000 CANADA	1	0	5
2004 CANADA	0	0	0
10 SEASONS	**4**	**1**	**104**
FWC QUALIFIERS	*0*	*0*	*0*

● ● ●

CONCACAF GOLD CUP QUALIFYING • Mauro Biello was part of the Canada squad that took part in Concacaf Gold Cup Qualifying in October 1999 against Cuba, El Salvador and Haiti. He made his competitive debut in the third match against Haiti, a 2-1 win that clinched Canada's berth in the 2000 Concacaf Gold

10

RIGHT BACK / DM

BOB BOLITHO

Born: 1952-07-20, Victoria, BC, CAN.   Height 178 cm. Dominant right foot.

1 Olympic Games: Group phase at Montréal 1976
2 cycles FIFA World Cup Qualifiers: 1976-77, 1980-81
1st #CANMNT: 1974-10-09 at Frankfurt, GER (v. DDR)
1st Goal: 1975-01-02 at Habana, CUB (v. CUB Jr.)

CANADA SOCCER HALL OF FAME

Bob Bolitho made 44 career international appearances for Canada, which ranked third all-time after his last match on 21 November 1981 in Tegucigalpa, Honduras. Across 10 years, he represented Canada in two cycles of FIFA World Cup Qualifiers as well as the 1975 Pan American Games in Mexico and Canada's home Olympic Games at Montréal 1976. He was part of the Canadian squad that came within a goal of qualifying for the 1982 FIFA World Cup in Spain.

Bolitho was just 22 years old when he made his 1974 Canada debut in a 2-0 loss to East Germany in Frankfurt. He scored his first goal in a January 1975 training match against Cuba's juniors, then scored his first official goal in August 1975 against Hungary at Montréal's Autostade. He scored against the Americans twice in 1976 FIFA World Cup Qualifiers: the 1-1 equaliser at Vancouver's Empire Stadium; and then the 3-0 goal on a free kick in a one-match playoff at Port-au-Prince, Haiti just three days before Christmas 1976.

Bolitho was an NASL Championship winner in 1979 with the Vancouver Whitecaps. In all, he played eight seasons in the NASL with the Whitecaps, Tulsa Roughnecks, Fort Lauderdale / Minnesota Strikers, and Tampa Bay Rowdies.

Bolitho got his start in the old Pacific Coast League with Victoria United O'Keefe in 1969-70. He also played in the Western Canada League, BC Premier League and BC League. In 1975, he won MVP honours at Canada Soccer's National Championships after leading Victoria's London Boxing AC to the national title.

CANADA RECORDS

INT'L RECORDS	MP	MS	MIN	G	A
1974 CANADA	6	6	496		
1975 CANADA	11	9	-	2g	
1976 CANADA	10	9	-	2g	
1977 CANADA	5	4	319		1a
1980 CANADA	8	8	-		1a
1981 CANADA	4	2	-	2g	2a
8 SEASONS	**44**	**38**	**n/a**	**6g**	**4a**
FWC QUALIFIERS	14	10	885	2g	1a

OLYMPIC GAMES	MP	MS	MIN		
1976 OLYMPIC	2	2	166		

1976 OLYMPIC GAMES • Bob Bolitho started both Canada matches at the 1976 Olympic Football Tournament, a narrow 2-1 loss to the Soviet Union in Montréal and a 3-1 loss to Korea DPR in Toronto. Of the 17 players selected to Canada's 1976 squad, Bolitho was the lone national amateur champion (1975) from before the Olympic Games.

GOALKEEPER

MILAN BORJAN

18

Born: 1987-10-23, Knin, YUG. Grew up in Hamilton, ON, CAN. Height 195 cm. Dominant right foot.

1 FIFA World Cup: Group phase at Qatar 2022
1 Concacaf medal: Silver in 2022-23 CNL
1st place FIFA World Cup Qualifiers in 2021-22
1st #CANMNT: 2011-02-09 at Larissa, GRE (v. GRE)
1st Clean Sheet: 2011-03-29 at Antalya, TUR (v. BLR)

CANADA HIGHLIGHTS

Milan Borjan is the Canada record holder with already 80 goalkeeper appearances and 35 clean sheets from February 2011 through December 2023. He has also made 19 Canada starts wearing the captain's armband. Across two years, he helped Canada finish in first place in the 2021-22 Concacaf Final Round of FIFA World Cup Qualifiers, featured in every Canada minute at the 2022 FIFA World Cup in Qatar, and won a Concacaf Silver Medal at the 2022-23 Nations League Finals.

Borjan has represented Canada in three cycles of FIFA World Cup Qualifiers and five editions of the Concacaf Gold Cup.

ŠK SLOVAN BRATISLAVA

Borjan joined ŠK Slovan Bratislava on loan ahead of the 2023-24 season in Slovakia. With Red Star Belgrade, he was a six-time Serbian SuperLiga winner and two-time Serbian Cup winner in six seasons from 2017-18 to 2022-23. He was the team's Athlete of the Year in 2018 and 2020.

In continental football, Borjan holds the record for all-time clean sheets by a Canadian in UEFA club competitions. He has already played 10 seasons in UEFA club competitions since 2014-15 with PFC Ludogrets, Red Star Belgrade and ŠK Slovan Bratislava.

CANADA RECORDS

"A" RECORDS		MP	MS	MIN	CS	
2011	CANADA	5	5	405	2	CS
2012	CANADA	4	2	204	2	CS
2013	CANADA	7	6	585	1	CS
2014	CANADA	5	5	450	1	CS
2015	CANADA	6	6	526	5	CS
2016	CANADA	5	5	382	0	CS
2017	CANADA	5	5	424	2	CS
2018	CANADA	3	3	270	3	CS
2019	CANADA	9	9	810	5	CS
2021	CANADA	9	9	810	5	CS
2022	CANADA	13	13	1170	6	CS
2023	CANADA	9	9	810	3	CS
UNTIL DEC.2023		80	77	6846	35	CS
FWC QUALIFIERS		24	23	2027	13	CS
GOLD CUP		15	15	1324	7	CS
NATIONS LEAGUE		12	12	1080	6	CS

FIFA WORLD CUP		MP	MS	MIN	CS	
2022	FIFA WC	3	3	270	0	CS

2022 FIFA WORLD CUP • Milan Borjan featured in every Canada minute at the FIFA World Cup in Qatar. In FIFA World Cup Qualifiers, he posted clean sheets against El Salvador (twice), Costa Rica, Honduras, USA and Jamaica, the last of which was that historic 4-0 win when Canada qualified for the men's FIFA World Cup for the first time in 36 years.

1

JACK BRAND

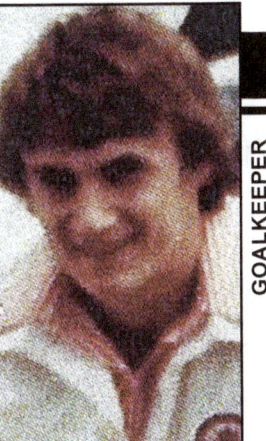

GOALKEEPER

Born: 1953-08-04, Braunschweig, GER. Height 185 cm.

1 Olympic Games: Group phase at Montréal 1976
1st #CANMNT: 1974-10-28 at Budapest, HUN (v. HUN U-23)
1st Clean Sheet: 1975-10-20 at Puebla, PB, MEX (v. JAM)

 CANADA SOCCER HALL OF FAME

Goalkeeper Jack Brand represented Canada at the 1975 Pan American Games in Mexico as well as Canada's home Olympic Games at Montréal 1976. Across four years, he made 15 career appearances including his international debut against Hungary's U-23 squad in Budapest. He posted his first international clean sheet in Canada's opening match at the 1975 Pan American Games, a 0-0 draw with Jamaica at Estadio Cuauhtémoc.

Brand was one of Canada's stars at the 1976 Olympic Games, notably sharing Players of the Match honours with captain Jimmy Douglas in the opener against the Soviet Union. Just three days before their Olympic opener, he was in goal for a 0-0 draw against France that was stopped after 60 minutes because of a thunderstorm.

Brand was an NASL Championship winner with the 1978 New York Cosmos, including the 2-1 win over the Tampa Bay Rowdies in the Final. He posted three clean sheets in five playoff matches that summer.

From 1974 to 1982, he played eight NASL seasons across nine years with the Toronto Metros / Metros-Croatia, Rochester Lancers, New York Cosmos, Tulsa Roughnecks, Seattle Sounders and Tampa Bay Rowdies. With Seattle, he was an NASL Second Team All-Star in 1980.

In 1976, he won the National League Ontario title with Toronto Italia FC. Before his pro career, he played at the University of Toronto.

CANADA RECORDS

INT'L RECORDS	MP	MS	MIN	CS
1974 CANADA	1	1	90	0 CS
1975 CANADA	8	8	675	1 CS
1976 CANADA	6	6	465	1 CS
3 SEASONS	**15**	**15**	**1230**	**2 CS**

OLYMPIC GAMES	MP	MS	MIN	CS
1976 OLYMPIC	2	2	180	0 CS

1976 OLYMPIC GAMES • Jack Brand was in goal for both Canada matches at the 1976 Olympic Football Tournament in Montréal and Toronto. Wrote coach Colin Morris after the 2-1 loss to the Soviet Union in the opener, "Brand made three reflex saves in one-on-one situations that had even Oleg Blokhin scratching his head."

LEFT BACK / LM

11

JIM BRENNAN

Born: 1977-05-08, East York, ON, CAN. Grew up in Newmarket, ON, CAN. Height 183 cm. Dominant left foot.

1 FIFA Confederations Cup: Group phase in 2001
1 Concacaf title: 2000 Concacaf Gold Cup
3 cycles FIFA World Cup Qualifiers: 2000, 2004, 2008
1st #CANMNT: 1999-04-27 at Belfast, NIR (v. NIR)
1st Goal: 1999-09-02 at Toronto, ON, CAN (v. JAM)

 CANADA SOCCER HALL OF FAME

Jim Brennan helped Canada win the 2000 Concacaf Gold and then participate in the FIFA Confederations Cup for the first time. From 1999 to 2008, he made 49 Canada appearances including three cycles of FIFA World Cup Qualifiers and three editions of the Concacaf Gold Cup.

In 2001, he featured in every Canada minute at the FIFA Confederations Cup in Japan, including a 0-0 draw against Brazil. He was named to the tournament's All-Star Team.

At the youth level, he represented Canada at the FIFA U-17 World Cup Japan 1993 and he won the 1996 Concacaf Youth Championship in Mexico.

From 2007 to 2010, Brennan played for Toronto FC in Major League Soccer. He was the team's MVP in 2007, featured in the 2008 MLS All-Star Game, and lifted the Voyageurs Cup in the 2009 Canadian Championship. He was the team's first captain in 2007.

Before coming home to Toronto, he played his football in England. He helped Bristol City FC win promotion from the Second Division in 1997-98 and then Norwich City FC win promotion from the First Division in 2003-04. He played with Norwich City FC in the Premier League in 2004-05.

CANADA RECORDS

"A" RECORDS	MP	MS	MIN	G	A
1999 CANADA	9	9	743	1g	1a
2000 CANADA	11	10	947	1g	
2001 CANADA	6	5	495		1a
2002 CANADA	5	5	510		1a
2003 CANADA	2	2	178	1g	1a
2004 CANADA	3	2	160	2g	2a
2005 CANADA	6	5	423		1a
2006 CANADA	1	0	45	1g	1a
2007 CANADA	1	1	90		
2008 CANADA	5	1	167		
10 SEASONS	**49**	**40**	**3758**	**6g**	**8a**
FWC QUALIFIERS	12	7	732	3g	2a
GOLD CUP	15	15	1401		2a

CONFEDERATIONS	MP	MS	MIN		
2001 FIFA CC	3	3	270		

1999 PLAYER OF THE YEAR • Jim Brennan was Canada's top player in 1999, the same year he made his international "A" debut against Northern Ireland, scored his first international goal against Jamaica, and got an assist on Canada's 2-1 match winner against Haiti to qualify for the 2000 Concacaf Gold Cup.

⑥

IAN BRIDGE

CENTRE BACK

Born: 1959-09-18, Victoria, BC, CAN.   Height 185 cm.
Dominant right foot.

1 FIFA World Cup: Group phase at Mexico 1986
1 Olympic Games: Quarterfinals at Los Angeles 1984
1 Concacaf title: 1985 Concacaf Championship
3 cycles FIFA World Cup Qualifiers: 1980-81, 1985, 1988
1st #CANMNT: 1981-10-12 at San Fernando, TRI (v. TRI)
1st Goal: 1981-11-12 at Tegucigalpa, HON (v. HON)

 CANADA SOCCER HALL OF FAME

Ian Bridge made 49 career international appearances for Canada from 1981 to 1991 including the Los Angeles 1984 Olympic Games and the FIFA World Cup Mexico 1986.

He helped Canada lift the Greg Kafaty Trophy at the 1985 Concacaf Championship when Canada qualified for the FIFA World Cup for the first time ever at King George V Park in St. John's. He was also in the Canada squad 17 months earlier when Canada qualified for the Olympic Games at Royal Athletic Park in Victoria.

After representing Canada at the 1979 FIFA World Youth Championship in Japan, Bridge made his international "A" debut on 12 October 1981 in San Fernando for a 4-2 away win over Trinidad and Tobago. He scored his first international goal exactly a month later in the Concacaf Final Round of FIFA World Cup Qualifiers at Tegucigalpa against Honduras. He scored his second goal just three days later, the 1-1 equaliser in a draw with Mexico.

Ian Bridge played his club soccer in Canada, England, USA and Switzerland. He played six seasons in the old NASL with the Seattle Sounders and Vancouver Whitecaps. He was an NASL playoff finalist in 1980 (injured) and 1982. He then moved to FC La Chaux-de-Fonds where he played in Switzerland before a short stint in the Canadian Soccer League.

CANADA RECORDS

INT'L RECORDS		MP	MS	MIN	G	A
1981	CANADA	6	5	-	2g	
1983	CANADA	7	7	585		
1984	CANADA	10	10	925	1g	
1985	CANADA	7	7	585		2a
1986	CANADA	5	5	405		
1988	CANADA	7	7	649	2g	
1989	CANADA	1	1	90		
1990	CANADA	2	2	135		
1991	CANADA	4	4	277		
11 SEASONS		**49**	**48**	**n/a**	**5g**	**2a**
FWC QUALIFIERS		12	12	1035	3g	2a
GOLD CUP		2	2	97		
3 NATIONS CUP		4	4	315		

FIFA / OLYMPIC		MP	MS	MIN
1984	OLYMPIC	4	4	390
1986	FIFA WC	3	3	270

1984 OLYMPIC GAMES • Ian Bridge helped Canada qualify for the Olympic Games in April 1984 with two matches played in his hometown Victoria. He helped Canada post three successive clean sheets, an away 0-0 draw with Costa Rica, a home 3-0 win over Cuba, and then the home 0-0 draw with Costa Rica to clinch a spot in the Olympic Games.

WING / FORWARD

TAJON BUCHANAN

Born: 1999-02-08, Toronto, ON, CAN. Grew up in Brampton, ON, CAN. Height 183 cm. Dominant right foot.

1 FIFA World Cup: Group phase at Qatar 2022
1 Concacaf medal: Silver in 2022-23 CNL
1st place FIFA World Cup Qualifiers in 2021-22
1st #CANMNT: 2021-06-05 at Bradenton, FL, USA (v. ARU)
1st Goal: 2021-07-29 at Houston, TX, USA (v. MEX)

CANADA HIGHLIGHTS

Tajon Buchanan was Canada's Player of the Match after he scored a goal and an assist against Jamaica in the historic 4-0 win that qualified Canada for the 2022 FIFA World Cup. In just three years, he has already reached the Concacaf Semifinals in 2021, won the Concacaf Final Round of FIFA World Cup Qualifiers in 2021-22, and won a Silver Medal in 2022-23 Concacaf Nations League.

At the U-23 level, Buchanan helped Canada climb to within a victory of the Tokyo Olympic Games by reaching the Semifinals at the 2021 Concacaf Olympic Qualifiers.

At the 2021 Concacaf Gold Cup, he won the Young Player Award as Canada reached the Semifinals for the first time in 14 years. He scored his first international goal in the Semifinals match against Mexico.

FC INTER MILAN

Buchanan became the first Canadian to feature in Italy's Serie A when he made his debut with FC Inter Milan in February 2024. He previously won the 2021-22 Championnat de Belgique with Club Brugge KV in his first European season and then reached the last 16 in UEFA Champions League in 2022-23.

In Major League Soccer with the New England Revolution, Buchanan was a 2021 MLS Supporters' Shield winner. He was 20 years old when he made his professional debut on 9 March 2019.

CANADA RECORDS

"A" RECORDS	MP	MS	MIN	G	A
2021 CANADA	16	12	1075	3g	4a
2022 CANADA	13	11	978	1g	2a
2023 CANADA	6	4	309		
UNTIL DEC.2023	35	27	2362	4g	6a
FWC QUALIFIERS	17	12	1120	3g	4a
GOLD CUP	5	5	435	1g	1a
NATIONS LEAGUE	8	6	475		

FIFA WORLD CUP	MP	MS	MIN	G	A
2022 FIFA WC	3	3	261		1a

2022 FIFA WORLD CUP • Tajon Buchanan featured in all three Canada matches at the FIFA World Cup in Qatar and he got the assist on the Men's National Team's historic first goal by Alphonso Davies in the second match. He led Canada with nine crosses in the tournament and produced their fastest runs against Belgium and Morocco.

⑨ ALEX BUNBURY

FORWARD

Born: 1967-06-18, Plaisance, GUY. Grew up in Montréal, QC, CAN. Height 186 cm. Dominant right foot.

3 cycles FIFA World Cup Qualifiers: 1988, 1992-93, 1996-97
1st #CANMNT: 1986-08-24 at Kallang, SIN (v. SIN)
1st "A" Goal: 1986-09-06 at Kallang, SIN (v. SIN)

 CANADA SOCCER HALL OF FAME

Alex Bunbury was Canada's record holder with 11 career goals in FIFA World Cup Qualifiers across three cycles from 1988 to 1997. He was Canada's top goalscorer across the 1992-93 and 1996-97 cycles and he retired with 16 career goals in 70 matches. He helped Canada reach the FIFA intercontinental playoff in 1993 and the Concacaf Final Round in 1997.

He also helped Canada win the 1988 Sir Stanley Matthews Cup in Toronto, played in the 1989 FIFA Futsal World Cup, and featured in two editions of the Concacaf Gold Cup.

After he represented Canada at the 1984 Concacaf Youth Championship and 1985 FIFA World Youth Championship, Bunbury made his international debut in Singapore just over eight weeks after the 1986 FIFA World Cup. Across his career, he scored away goals in FIFA World Cup Qualifiers at Tegucigalpa's Estadio Tiburcio Carías Andino, México City's Estadio Azteca, and San Salvador's Estadio Cuscatlán.

Bunbury was a club legend at CS Marítimo where he led the club in goalscoring for four-straight seasons and reached the Taça de Portugal Final in 1995. After his return to North America, he won the 2000 MLS Cup with Kansas City.

In Canada, he was 19 years old when he made his pro debut on 14 June 1987. In England, he helped West Ham United FC earn promotion to the Premier League for the 1993-94 season.

CANADA RECORDS

"A" RECORDS		MP	MS	MIN	G	A
1986	CANADA	5	5	440	1g	
1987	CANADA	3	2	-	1g	
1988	CANADA	7	4	461		
1989	CANADA	4	4	360		1a
1992	CANADA	11	9	-	3g	1a
1993	CANADA	12	12	1099	4g	2a
1995	CANADA	4	4	358	1g	1a
1996	CANADA	9	8	750	3g	1a
1997	CANADA	10	10	866	2g	
1999	CANADA	0	0	0		
14 SEASONS		**65**	**58**	**n/a**	**15g**	**6a**
FWC QUALIFIERS		*31*	*30*	*2723*	*11g*	*3a*
GOLD CUP		*5*	*4*	*405*	*1g*	*1a*

PLAYER OF THE YEAR • Alex Bunbury was Canada Soccer's inaugural Player of the Year in 1993 before he won the award for the second time in 1995. He led Canada with six goals in the 1992-93 FIFA World Cup Qualifiers campaign. He also joined West Ham United FC in their promotion run to the Premier League.

FORWARD

JOHN CATLIFF

10

Born: 1965-01-08, Vancouver, BC, CAN. Height 190 cm. Dominant left foot.

Missed FIFA World Cup in 1986 through injury
1 Olympic Games: Quarterfinals at Los Angeles 1984
1 Concacaf title: 1985 Concacaf Championship
3 cycles FIFA World Cup Qualifiers: 1985, 1988, 1992-93
1st #CANMNT: 1984-06-23 at Guangzhou, CHN (v. NGA)
1st Goal: 1984-06-23 at Guangzhou, Canton, CHN (v. NGA)

CANADA SOCCER HALL OF FAME

John Catliff was Canada's record holder with 26 international goals scored across 60 matches in 11 years from 1984 to 1994. He led Canada in goals scored during the 1993 Concacaf Final Round of FIFA World Cup Qualifiers and finished his career ranked second with 18 goals in international "A" matches.

He helped Canada reach the Quarterfinals at the 1984 Olympic Games and win the 1985 Concacaf Championship. An injury in Honduras prevented him from competing in Canada's qualification match at King George V Park in St. John's as well as the 1986 FIFA World Cup in Mexico.

Catliff was just 19 years old when he scored two goals in his international debut against Nigeria at the 1984 Great Wall Championship. He scored five goals in four matches in that tournament before the Olympic Games. He scored his first international "A" goal a year later at the President's Cup, albeit in a 6-1 loss to the Arabian Gulf Cup champions Iraq.

Catliff was a five-time CSL Championship winner, once with the Calgary Kickers (1987) and four times with the Vancouver 86ers (1988 to 1991). He was a two-time CSL Golden Boot winner and MVP of the 1988 season.

After his college career at Harvard University, Catliff made his pro debut on 7 June 1987 with the Calgary Kickers.

CANADA RECORDS

INT'L RECORDS		MP	MS	MIN	G	A
1984	CANADA	6	4	-	5g	
1985	CANADA	3	2	-	1g	
1987	CANADA	7	6	-	1g	2a
1988	CANADA	14	14	-	7g	2a
1990	CANADA	2	2	169	3g	
1991	CANADA	4	4	344		1a
1992	CANADA	9	8	-	3g	1a
1993	CANADA	10	9	803	6g	1a
1994	CANADA	5	1	219		
11 SEASONS		**60**	**50**	**n/a**	**26g**	**7a**
FWC QUALIFIERS		13	12	882	4g	2a
3 NATIONS CUP		4	4	333	3g	

FIFA / OLYMPIC		MP	MS	MIN		
1984	OLYMPIC	1	0	29		
1986	FIFA WC	INJ	-	-		

● ● ●

THREE NATIONS CUP • John Catliff was Canada's star player when they won the 1990 North American Championship in Burnaby, British Columbia. In the round-robin competition, he scored the 1-0 match winner against the United States and both goals in a 2-1 win over Mexico to clinch the title.

LUCAS CAVALLINI

FORWARD

Born: 1992-12-28, Toronto, ON, CAN. Grew up in Mississauga, ON, CAN. Height 180 cm. Dominant left foot.

1 FIFA World Cup: Group phase at Qatar 2022
1 Concacaf medal: Silver in 2022-23 CNL
1st place FIFA World Cup Qualifiers in 2021-22
1st #CANMNT: 2012-08-15 at Lauderhill, FL, USA (v. TRI)
1st Goal: 2018-08-09 at Bradenton, FL, USA (v. VIR)

CANADA HIGHLIGHTS

Lucas Cavallini was a Canada record holder when he shared the Men's National Team mark for international goals in a year (eight goals in 2019). Through December 2023, he has already scored 19 goals in 40 international "A" appearances, including hat tricks against Cuba in 2019 and Cayman Islands in 2021. He helped Canada finish in first place in the 2021-22 Concacaf Final Round of FIFA World Cup Qualifiers, featured at the 2022 FIFA World Cup in Qatar, and won a Concacaf Silver Medal at the 2022-23 Concacaf Nations League Finals.

He scored two of his biggest goals in 2019 against Mexico at the Concacaf Gold Cup and against USA in a home Concacaf Nations League match at Toronto's BMO Field, the latter of which helped Canada secure their first international victory over the Americans in 34 years.

At the U-23 level, Cavallini helped Canada climb to within a victory of the London 2012 Olympic Games by reaching the Semifinals at the Concacaf Olympic Qualifiers.

PUEBLA FC

Cavallini rejoined Puebla FC in January 2024. He played three seasons at Vancouver Whitecaps FC and won the Canadian Championship in 2022. He was the team's Domenic Mobilio Golden Boot winner in 2020. He started his professional career in Uruguay.

CANADA RECORDS

"A" RECORDS	MP	MS	MIN	G	A
2012 CANADA	2	0	40		
2015 CANADA	1	0	45		
2017 CANADA	4	2	217		1a
2018 CANADA	3	3	174	3g	
2019 CANADA	7	5	421	8g	
2020 CANADA	0	0	0		
2021 CANADA	11	4	427	5g	1a
2022 CANADA	7	2	237	2g	
2023 CANADA	5	4	327	1g	1a
UNTIL DEC.2023	40	20	1888	19g	3a
FWC QUALIFIERS	11	3	341	5g	
GOLD CUP	16	11	998	6g	3a
NATIONS LEAGUE	4	1	113	2g	

FIFA WORLD CUP	MP	MS	MIN		
2022 FIFA WC	1	0	18		

2022 FIFA WORLD CUP • Lucas Cavallini made his FIFA World Cup debut in Canada's second group match at Qatar 2022. He came in as a substitute in the loss to Croatia. In Canada's last preparation match before the tournament, he scored the 2-1 match winner from the penalty spot against Japan.

GOALKEEPER

TONY CHURSKY

Born: 1953-06-13, New Westminster, BC, CAN. Height 180 cm.

3 cycles FIFA World Cup Qualifiers: 1972, 1976-77, 1980
1st #CANMNT: 1973-08-01 at Toronto, ON, CAN (v. POL)
1st Clean Sheet: 1973-09-30 at Valletta, MLT (v. MLT "B")

CANADA SOCCER HALL OF FAME

Tony Chursky made 27 international appearances for Canada, ranked first amongst goalkeepers after his last Canada match on 14 October 1981. He was selected to represent Canada in three cycles of FIFA World Cup Qualifiers, most notably 1976-77 when Canada finished in fourth place.

Chursky was just 20 years old when he made his international "A" debut on 1 August 1973 in front of a record Canada crowd at Toronto's Varsity Stadium, a 3-1 loss to Poland who were less than a year away from a third-place finish at the 1974 FIFA World Cup. He posted his first "A" clean sheet in a 1-0 away win over Haiti at Stade Sylvio Cator on 12 November 1974.

Chursky played seven seasons in the old NASL with the Seattle Sounders, California Surf, Chicago Sting and Toronto Blizzard. He had his best years in Seattle where he reached the NASL Final in 1977. Beyond his playing career, he was named to Seattle's All-Time NASL Team in 2014.

After the NASL folded, Chursky played in the MISL with the indoor Tacoma Stars.

Before turning pro in 1976, Chursky played in the Pacific Coast League, Western Canada League, BC Premier League and BC League. He won a Canada Games Gold Medal in 1973.

In 1970-71, Chursky was still just 18 years old when he broke into the Pacific Coast League with Croatia SC Vancouver to replace injured goalkeeper Greg Weber. He helped the team win the Top Star Trophy in the playoffs.

CANADA RECORDS

INT'L RECORDS	MP	MS	MIN	CS
1972 CANADA	0	0	0	0 CS
1973 CANADA	4	4	360	2 CS
1974 CANADA	6	6	540	1 CS
1975 CANADA	3	3	270	1 CS
1976 CANADA	4	4	360	2 CS
1977 CANADA	5	5	405	0 CS
1980 CANADA	3	3	270	1 CS
1981 CANADA	2	0	90	0 CS
10 SEASONS	**27**	**25**	**2295**	**7 CS**
FWC QUALIFIERS	*8*	*8*	*675*	*2 CS*

● ● ●

FIFA WORLD CUP QUALIFIERS • Tony Chursky was at his best in 1976-77 FIFA World Cup Qualifiers when Canada finished fourth in the region. In 1976, he posted clean sheets and earned Player of the Match honours in both a 1-0 home win over Mexico at Vancouver and a 0-0 away draw against Mexico at Toluca.

CARLO CORAZZIN

Born: 1971-12-25, New Westminster, BC, CAN. Grew up in Coquitlam, BC, CAN. Height 180 cm. Dominant right foot.

1 FIFA Confederations Cup: Group phase in 2001
1 Concacaf title: 2000 Concacaf Gold Cup
3 cycles FIFA World Cup Qualifiers: 1996-97, 2000, 2004
1st #CANMNT "A": 1994-06-01 at Montréal, QC, CAN (v. MAR)
1st Goal: 1996-01-10 at Anaheim, CA, USA (v. HON)

 CANADA SOCCER HALL OF FAME

Carlo Corazzin was the Top Scorer at the 2000 Concacaf Gold Cup when Canada lifted their second men's confederation title and qualified for the FIFA Confederations Cup for the first time. From 1992 to 2004, he played in three cycles of FIFA World Cup Qualifiers and three editions of the Concacaf Gold Cup. He was 17 years old when he helped Canada win the 1989 Jeux de la Francophonie in Morocco.

He scored four goals at the 2000 Concacaf Gold Cup: two goals against Costa Rica in the group phase; the late equaliser before a 2-1 win over Mexico in the Quarterfinals; and the 2-0 goal against Colombia in the Concacaf Final.

Corazzin was a CSL Championship winner with the Winnipeg Fury in 1992. He then helped the Vancouver 86ers win the APSL regular season title in 1993. From there, he played in England from 1994-95 to 2002-03 with Cambridge United, Plymouth Argyle, Northampton Town and Oldham Athletic. He helped Northampton Town FC earn promotion in 1999-2000. He played his last three pro seasons in Canada with Vancouver Whitecaps FC.

Corazzin played his youth soccer in British Columbia before he moved to Italy where he played in Serie D and Serie C as a teenager.

CANADA RECORDS

"A" RECORDS		MP	MS	MIN	G	A
1992	CANADA	0	0	0		
1994	CANADA	5	5	265		
1995	CANADA	6	6	528		
1996	CANADA	8	5	546	2g	
1997	CANADA	9	7	591	1g	
1999	CANADA	4	3	246	3g	
2000	CANADA	17	17	1389	4g	2a
2001	CANADA	5	3	267		
2003	CANADA	3	1	95		
2004	CANADA	2	1	94	1g	
13 SEASONS		**59**	**48**	**4021**	**11g**	**2a**
FWC QUALIFIERS		*23*	*17*	*1526*	*2g*	*1a*
GOLD CUP		*9*	*7*	*649*	*5g*	*1a*

CONFEDERATIONS		MP	MS	MIN
2001	FIFA CC	3	1	132

2001 FIFA CONFEDERATIONS CUP • Carlo Corazzin featured in all three Canada matches in Japan at the 2001 FIFA Confederations Cup. He was a substitute in the loss to Japan, he played the second half of a 0-0 draw with Brazil, and he was a starter in the 2-0 loss to Cameroon.

GOALKEEPER

MAXIME CRÉPEAU

16

Born: 1994-05-11, Greenfield Park, QC, CAN. Grew up in Candiac, QC, CAN. Height 185 cm. Dominant right foot.

Missed FIFA World Cup in 2022 through injury
1st place FIFA World Cup Qualifiers in 2021-22
1st #CANMNT: 2016-02-05 at Carson, CA, USA (v. USA)
1st Clean Sheet: 2021-03-29 at Bradenton, FL, USA (v. CAY)

CANADA HIGHLIGHTS

Maxime Crépeau helped Canada qualify for the 2022 FIFA World Cup and win the 2021-22 Concacaf Final Round of FIFA World Cup Qualifiers, but he missed the final competition in Qatar through injury.

In 2021, he featured in every Canada minute at the Concacaf Gold Cup when Canada reached the Semifinals for the first time in 14 years. He notably saved a penalty attempt from Mexico's Carlos Salcedo in the Semifinals (a 2-1 loss a.e.t.).

At the youth level, Crépeau represented Canada at the FIFA U-17 World Cup Mexico 2011. At the U-23 level, he helped Canada reach the Concacaf Olympic Qualifiers Semifinals, getting to within a win over qualifying for Rio 2016.

PORTLAND TIMBERS FC

Crépeau won both the 2022 MLS Supporters' Shield and MLS Cup with LAFC, but he was badly injured in the Final which caused him to miss the FIFA World Cup. He returned to action in 2023 and reached the MLS Cup Final for the second year in a row.

He was Ottawa's Player of the Year in 2018 and Vancouver's Player of the Year in both 2019 and 2021. He was also the USL-1 Goalkeeper of the Year in 2018. He previously played for the Montréal Impact and was a Canadian Championship winner in 2013.

CANADA RECORDS

"A" RECORDS	MP	MS	MIN	CS
2014 CANADA	0	0	0	0 CS
2015 CANADA	0	0	0	0 CS
2016 CANADA	1	1	90	0 CS
2017 CANADA	1	0	26	0 CS
2018 CANADA	0	0	0	0 CS
2019 CANADA	0	0	0	0 CS
2020 CANADA	3	3	270	0 CS
2021 CANADA	9	9	810	3 CS
2022 CANADA	1	1	90	0 CS
2023 CANADA	INJ	0	0	0 CS
UNTIL DEC.2023	15	14	1286	3 CS
FWC QUALIFIERS	5	5	450	2 CS
GOLD CUP	6	5	476	1 CS
NATIONS LEAGUE	0	0	0	0 CS
FIFA WORLD CUP	**MP**	**MS**	**MIN**	**CS**
2022 FIFA WC	INJ	-	-	

FIFA WORLD CUP QUALIFIERS • Maxime Crépeau made five appearances in goal for Canada during 2021-22 FIFA World Cup Qualifiers when they qualified for Qatar 2022. In an important October 2021 window, he was in goal for a 1-1 draw at Estadio Azteca, a 0-0 draw at Jamaica's National Stadium, and a 4-1 win over Panama in Toronto.

NICK DASOVIĆ

Born: 1968-12-05, Vancouver, BC, CAN. Height 185 cm. Dominant right foot.

1 FIFA Confederations Cup: Group phase in 2001
3 cycles FIFA World Cup Qualifiers: 1992-93, 1996-97, 2000
1st #CANMNT: 1992-04-02 at Victoria, BC, CAN (v. CHN)
1st Goal: 1993-07-11 at México, DF, MEX (v. CRC)

CANADA SOCCER HALL OF FAME

Nick Dasović was twice Canada's runner up in Player of the Year voting, featured in two matches at the 2001 FIFA Confederations Cup, and won a Concacaf Bronze Medal at the 2002 Concacaf Gold Cup. He helped Canada reach FIFA's intercontinental playoff in 1993 and the Concacaf Final Round in 1997. He also featured in Canada's 1994 historic 1-1 draw with Brazil in front of a Canadian record crowd at Edmonton's Commonwealth Stadium.

He scored his first international goal at famous Estadio Azteca, the opening goal of a 1-1 draw with Costa Rica at the 1993 Concacaf Gold Cup. He scored his second international goal in 1996 in FIFA World Cup Qualifiers at Edmonton.

He won the 1994 APSL Championship with the Montréal Impact and the 1996-97 Scottish First Division with St. Johnstone FC. As a teenager, he helped Croatia SC Vancouver finish second at Canada Soccer's 1986 National Championships.

After he moved to Europe where he reached the Yugoslavian First Division, he then played in the Canadian Soccer League with the North York Rockets and APSL with Montréal and Vancouver. He returned to Europe where he played in France, Sweden and Scotland.

CANADA RECORDS

"A" RECORDS	MP	MS	MIN	G	A
1992 CANADA	7	7	630		2a
1993 CANADA	8	6	545	1g	
1994 CANADA	5	5	408		
1995 CANADA	6	5	387		1a
1996 CANADA	7	5	447	1g	
1997 CANADA	2	2	145		
1999 CANADA	10	10	799		
2000 CANADA	4	4	315		
2001 CANADA	5	5	360		
2002 CANADA	4	4	390		
2003 CANADA	4	4	345		
2004 CANADA	1	1	90		
13 SEASONS	**63**	**58**	**4861**	**2g**	**3a**
FWC QUALIFIERS	17	15	1285	1g	
GOLD CUP	8	8	750	1g	

CONFEDERATIONS	MP	MS	MIN
2001 FIFA CC	2	2	180

2001 FIFA CONFEDERATIONS CUP • Nick Dasović featured in two Canada matches in Japan at the 2001 FIFA Confederations Cup: a memorable 0-0 draw with Brazil and a 2-0 loss to Cameroon. In October 1999, he helped Canada qualify for the 2000 Concacaf Gold Cup, but then he missed the tournament four months later through injury.

FORWARD

20

JONATHAN DAVID

Born: 2000-01-14, Brooklyn, NY, USA. Grew up in Ottawa, ON, CAN. Height 175 cm. Dominant right foot.

1 FIFA World Cup: Group phase at Qatar 2022
1 Concacaf medal: Silver in 2022-23 CNL
1st place FIFA World Cup Qualifiers in 2021-22
1st #CANMNT: 2018-09-09 at Bradenton, FL, USA (v. VIR)
1st Two Goals: 2018-09-09 at Bradenton, FL, USA (v. VIR)

CANADA HIGHLIGHTS

Jonathan David was a Canada record holder when he shared the Men's National Team mark for international goals in a year (eight goals in 2019). Through December 2023, he has already scored 26 goals in 45 matches, including hat tricks against Cuba in 2019 and Suriname in 2021.

He helped Canada finish in first place in the 2021-22 Concacaf Final Round of FIFA World Cup Qualifiers, played in all three Canada matches at the 2022 FIFA World Cup, and won a Silver Medal in 2022-23 Concacaf Nations League.

In 2019, David won Canada Soccer's Player of the Year award in 2019 as well as the Concacaf Gold Cup Top Scorer Award. He scored a highlight-reel goal against Cuba in Concacaf Nations League.

In 2021-22 FIFA World Cup Qualifiers, he scored a big match winner against Costa Rica in front of 48,806 fans at Edmonton's Commonwealth Stadium, then scored in away victories against both El Salvador and Honduras.

LILLE OSC

David led Lille OSC to the 2020-21 Ligue 1 title in his first year in France, an impressive season in which he broke the record for most goals by a Canadian in a top-5 European league. He scored 13 goals in 2020-21, but improved to 24 goals in 2022-23. Before moving to France, he was the Championnat de Belgique's joint top goalscorer in 2019-20 with 18 goals for second-place KAA Gent.

CANADA RECORDS

"A" RECORDS	MP	MS	MIN	G	A
2018 CANADA	3	2	140	3g	2a
2019 CANADA	9	8	703	8g	3a
2020 CANADA	0	0	0		
2021 CANADA	12	9	821	7g	4a
2022 CANADA	14	12	1053	4g	2a
2023 CANADA	7	7	617	4g	2a
UNTIL DEC.2023	45	38	3334	26g	13a
FWC QUALIFIERS	18	15	1345	9g	5a
GOLD CUP	4	3	303	6g	2a
NATIONS LEAGUE	12	11	934	6g	3a

FIFA WORLD CUP	MP	MS	MIN
2022 FIFA WC	3	2	192

● ● ●

2022 FIFA WORLD CUP • Jonathan David featured in all three Canada matches at the FIFA World Cup in Qatar, including starts against both Belgium and Croatia. In the opening match against Belgium, David led Canada with seven attempts on target, 87 offers to receive in actions off the ball, and an exhausting 12.36 kilometres covered in distance.

19

ALPHONSO DAVIES

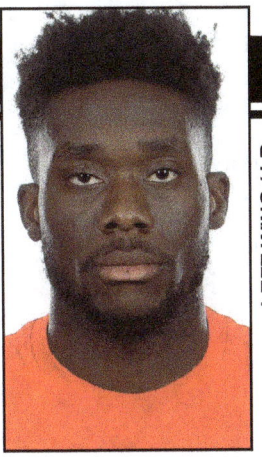

LEFT WING / LB

Born: 2000-11-20, Gomoa Buduburam, GHA. Grew up in Edmonton, AB, CAN. Height 178 cm. Dominant left foot.

1 FIFA World Cup: Group phase at Qatar 2022
1 Concacaf medal: Silver in 2022-23 CNL
1st place FIFA World Cup Qualifiers in 2021-22
1st #CANMNT: 2017-06-13 at Montréal, QC, CAN (v. CUW)
1st Goal: 2017-07-07 at Harrison, NJ, USA (v. GUF)

CANADA HIGHLIGHTS

Alphonso Davies featured in every Canada minute at the 2022 FIFA World Cup in Qatar where he also became Canada's first goalscorer at the men's FIFA World Cup. He has already helped Canada finish in first place in the 2021-22 Concacaf Final Round of FIFA World Cup Qualifiers and won a Concacaf Silver Medal at the 2022-23 Nations League Finals. Through December 2023, he has scored 15 goals and holds the Canada record with 17 assists.

Davies was just 16 years old when he became Canada's youngest debutant on 13 June 2017 at Montréal's Stade Saputo. That summer, he scored his first three goals and won the Best Young Player Award at the Concacaf Gold Cup. In 2019, he scored the match winner when Canada beat USA for the first time in 34 years.

In 2021-22 FIFA World Cup Qualifiers, he got the assist on Canada's 1-1 away equalisers against both USA and Mexico, then scored a highlight-reel match winner against Panama at Toronto's BMO Field.

FC BAYERN MÜNCHEN

Davies was the first Canadian to win the men's UEFA Champions League and the FIFA Club World Cup. Named to the FIFA FIFPro World 11 in 2020, he was the second Canadian to win both the Bundesliga and German Cup. Before he moved to Germany, he made his MLS debut in 2016 at age 15. He won Vancouver's Player of the Year award in 2018.

CANADA RECORDS

"A" RECORDS	MP	MS	MIN	G	A
2017 CANADA	6	3	371	3g	
2018 CANADA	3	3	270		4a
2019 CANADA	8	8	644	2g	3a
2020 CANADA	0	0	0		
2021 CANADA	13	12	1058	5g	8a
2022 CANADA	7	7	586	3g	1a
2023 CANADA	7	6	528	2g	1a
UNTIL DEC.2023	44	39	3457	15g	17a
FWC QUALIFIERS	13	12	1058	5g	8a
GOLD CUP	8	7	577	3g	3a
NATIONS LEAGUE	12	11	929	6g	1a

FIFA WORLD CUP	MP	MS	MIN	G
2022 FIFA WC	3	3	270	1g

PLAYER OF THE YEAR • Alphonso Davies won Canada Soccer's Player of the Year award four times in five years from 2018 to 2022. He was also a two-time Canadian Athlete of the Year (2018, 2020). He was the Bundesliga Rookie of the Season in 2019-20 and he was named to the FIFA FIFPro Men's World11 in 2020.

MIDFIELDER

JULIAN DE GUZMAN

Born: 1981-03-25, Scarborough, ON, CAN. Height 170 cm. Dominant right foot.

4 cycles FIFA WC Qualifiers: 2004, 2008, 2012, 2015-16
1st #CANMNT: 2002-01-26 at Miami, FL, USA (v. MTQ)
1st Goal: 2007-06-06 at Miami, FL, USA (v. CRC)

CANADA HIGHLIGHTS

Julian de Guzman was a Canada record holder with 89 international "A" appearances from 2002 to 2016. He made 25 Canada starts wearing the captain's armband, featured in four cycles of FIFA World Cup Qualifiers, and reached the Concacaf Gold Cup Semifinals in both 2002 and 2007. He was the MVP of the Concacaf Gold Cup in 2007 and Canada Soccer's Player of the Year in 2008.

At the 2007 Concacaf Gold Cup, he scored his first two international goals in a come-from-behind 2-1 win over Costa Rica in the group phase. The following year in a 2008 friendly at Seattle, he scored the 2-2 goal in a 3-2 loss to Brazil, the reigning Copa América champions.

CLUB HIGHLIGHTS

He played three seasons in the German Bundesliga with Hannover 96 and four seasons in Spain's La Liga with Deportivo La Coruña where he was named his team's 2007-08 Player of the Season. After playing his youth soccer in Canada, he moved to France in 1997 where he joined Olympique de Marseille B and to Germany in 2000 where he joined 1.FC Saarbrücken.

Back home with Toronto FC, he was a three-time Canadian Championship winner from 2010 to 2012.

CANADA RECORDS

"A" RECORDS	MP	MS	MIN	G	A
2002 CANADA	4	1	117		
2003 CANADA	2	2	180		
2004 CANADA	7	7	569		
2005 CANADA	2	2	180		
2006 CANADA	3	3	191		1a
2007 CANADA	10	10	872	2g	4a
2008 CANADA	7	7	576	2g	
2009 CANADA	7	7	580		
2010 CANADA	2	2	180		
2011 CANADA	8	7	667		1a
2012 CANADA	9	9	774		1a
2013 CANADA	8	8	578		
2014 CANADA	5	5	422		
2015 CANADA	11	11	827		
2016 CANADA	4	3	229		
15 SEASONS	**89**	**84**	**6942**	**4g**	**7a**
FWC QUALIFIERS	29	29	2321	1g	
GOLD CUP	17	15	1347	2g	3a

● ● ●

PLAYER OF THE YEAR • Julian de Guzman was Canada Soccer's Player of the Year in 2008, the same year he won 2007-08 Player of the Season honours with Deportivo La Coruña. He scored two international goals that year, a spectacular right-footed blast from distance against Brazil and his first FIFA World Cup Qualifiers goal against Jamaica.

17

MARCEL DE JONG

LEFT BACK

Born: 1986-10-15, Newmarket, ON, CAN. Grew up in Valkenswaard, NED. Height 175 cm. Dominant left foot.

3 cycles FIFA World Cup Qualifiers: 2008, 2012, 2015-16
1st #CANMNT: 2007-11-20 at Durban, RSA (v. RSA)
1st Goal: 2009-07-10 at Miami, FL, USA (v. CRC)

CANADA HIGHLIGHTS

Marcel de Jong made 56 career international "A" appearances for Canada from 2007 to 2018, including three cycles of FIFA World Cup Qualifiers and five editions of the Concacaf Gold Cup. He helped Canada reach the Concacaf Gold Cup Quarterfinals in both 2009 and 2017 and he wore the captain's armband for his milestone 50th international match in January 2017.

As a teen, de Jong represented Canada at the FIFA World Youth Championship Netherlands 2005. Just over two years later, he made his international "A" debut on 20 November 2007 in South Africa. In 2015-16 FIFA World Cup Qualifiers, de Jong co-led Canada with 540 minutes.

CLUB HIGHLIGHTS

He played his professional football in Netherlands, Germany, USA and Canada, notably helping FC Augsburg win promotion in 2010-11 from the 2.Bundesliga. He then played three-plus seasons in the Bundesliga before he moved to Major League Soccer. In the Netherlands, he played four seasons in the Eredivisie with Roda JC.

He helped Sporting Kansas City win the 2015 US Open Cup and Vancouver Whitecaps FC reach the 2016-17 Concacaf Champions League Semifinals. He also helped Whitecaps FC finish as runners up in the 2018 Canadian Championship.

CANADA RECORDS

"A" RECORDS	MP	MS	MIN	G	A
2007 CANADA	1	0	17		
2008 CANADA	6	4	275		
2009 CANADA	6	4	277	1g	1a
2010 CANADA	2	2	120		
2011 CANADA	2	2	180		
2012 CANADA	3	1	140		1a
2013 CANADA	9	9	643		
2014 CANADA	2	2	165	1g	
2015 CANADA	10	10	796	1g	
2016 CANADA	8	8	668		
2017 CANADA	6	6	495		
2018 CANADA	1	0	29		
12 SEASONS	56	48	3805	3g	2a
FWC QUALIFIERS	14	12	1013		
GOLD CUP	13	12	1012	1g	

1st INTERNATIONAL GOAL • Marcel de Jong scored his first international goal at the 2009 Concacaf Gold Cup, a fantastic left-footed shot that helped Canada clinch first place in Group A ahead of Costa Rica. He later scored international goals in friendly matches against Jamaica (2014) and Ghana (2015).

ATTACKING MID / F

DWAYNE DE ROSARIO

Born: 1978-05-15, Scarborough, ON, CAN. Height 178 cm. Dominant right foot.

1 FIFA Confederations Cup: Group phase in 2001
1 Concacaf title: 2000 Concacaf Gold Cup
4 cycles FIFA World Cup Qualifiers: 2000, 2004, 2008, 2011-12
1st #CANMNT: 1998-05-18 at Toronto, ON, CAN (v. MKD)
1st Goal: 2002-02-02 at Pasadena, CA, USA (v. KOR)

 **CANADA SOCCER HALL OF FAME**

Dwayne De Rosario was Canada's record holder with 22 international "A" goals across 20 years of football from 1996 to 2015. He was a Concacaf Gold Cup champion in 2000 and four-time Canada Soccer Player of the Year. He also represented Canada at the FIFA Confederations Cup Korea/Japan 2001.

After winning the 1996 Concacaf Youth Championship and reaching the knockout phase at the 1997 FIFA World Youth Championship in Malaysia, De Rosario made his international "A" debut at age 20 on 18 May 1998 against FYR Macedonia at Toronto's Varsity Stadium.

He was a four-time MLS Cup winner and one-time MLS Supporters' Shield winner with the San Jose Earthquakes / Houston Dynamo from 2001 to 2008. He was MVP of the MLS Cup in both 2001 and 2007 as well as MVP of the 2006 MLS All-Star Game. He then won the George Gross Trophy twice as MVP of the Canadian Championship in 2009 and 2010 with Toronto FC. He won MLS MVP honours in 2011 in a year split between three teams.

CANADA RECORDS

"A" RECORDS	MP	MS	MIN	G	A
1996 CANADA	0	0	0		
1997 CANADA	0	0	0		
1998 CANADA	1	0	36		
1999 CANADA	2	1	63		
2000 CANADA	2	0	40		
2001 CANADA	4	0	101		
2002 CANADA	7	3	397	2g	1a
2003 CANADA	1	0	45	1g	1a
2004 CANADA	10	10	878	4g	3a
2005 CANADA	8	8	703		2a
2006 CANADA	2	2	180		
2007 CANADA	8	8	676	5g	
2008 CANADA	8	8	709	3g	4a
2010 CANADA	2	2	178		
2011 CANADA	11	11	908	4g	2a
2012 CANADA	5	5	369	1g	
2013 CANADA	6	6	423		
2014 CANADA	2	1	83		
2015 CANADA	2	1	102	2g	
20 SEASONS	**81**	**66**	**5891**	**22g**	**13a**
FWC QUALIFIERS	24	23	1944	9g	8a
GOLD CUP	17	12	1197	6g	

CONFEDERATIONS	MP	MS	MIN		
2001 FIFA CC	2	0	51		

PLAYER OF THE YEAR • Dwayne De Rosario was the first Men's National Team Player to win Canada Soccer Player of the Year honours four times. He won the award three years in a row from 2005 to 2007, then won it again in 2011 when he also won Most Valuable Player honours in Major League Soccer for the first time.

5

JASON DEVOS

CENTRE BACK

Born: 1974-01-12, London, ON, CAN. Grew up in Appin, ON, CAN. Height 187 cm. Dominant right foot.

1 FIFA Confederations Cup: Group phase in 2001
1 Concacaf title: 2000 Concacaf Gold Cup
3 cycles FIFA World Cup Qualifiers: 1997, 2000, 2004
1st #CANMNT: 1997-08-17 at Toronto, ON, CAN (v. IRN)
1st Goal: 1999-06-02 at Edmonton, AB, CAN (v. GUA)

 CANADA SOCCER HALL OF FAME

Jason deVos was Canada's captain when they lifted the 2000 Concacaf Gold Cup and featured at the 2001 FIFA Confederations Cup in Japan. From 1999 to 2004, he made more than 30 starts wearing the captain's armband.

As a youth player, he represented Canada at the 1992 Concacaf Youth Championship and 1996 Concacaf Olympic Qualifiers. He was 23 years old when made his international "A" debut on 17 August 1997 in Toronto.

At the 2000 Concacaf Gold, he scored the match winner in Canada's 2-0 win over Colombia in the Final, a header late in the first half from a Martin Nash corner kick.

He played 12 seasons in England and Scotland, breaking in with Darlington FC in 1996-97. He helped Wigan Athletic win the 2002-03 Second Division to earn a promotion to the First Division. A year later, he joined Ipswich Town FC where he played his last four seasons including a third-place finish in the Championship in 2004-05.

Before moving to Europe, deVos won the 1994 APSL Championship and 1996 Commissioner's Cup with Montréal. He played in the Canadian Soccer League with the London Lasers and Kitchener Kickers. He was just 16 years old when he made his pro debut on 18 July 1990.

CANADA RECORDS

"A" RECORDS	MP	MS	MIN	G	A
1996 CANADA	0	0	0		
1997 CANADA	3	2	225		
1998 CANADA	1	1	90		
1999 CANADA	10	10	895	1g	2a
2000 CANADA	14	14	1257	2g	1a
2001 CANADA	4	4	360		
2002 CANADA	6	6	600		
2003 CANADA	5	5	414		
2004 CANADA	6	6	540	1g	2a
9 SEASONS	**49**	**48**	**4381**	**4g**	**5a**
FWC QUALIFIERS	*13*	*12*	*1125*	*2g*	*2a*
GOLD CUP	*12*	*12*	*1142*	*1g*	*1a*

CONFEDERATIONS	MP	MS	MIN
2001 FIFA CC	3	3	270

2001 FIFA CONFEDERATIONS CUP • Jason deVos was Canada's captain at the 2001 FIFA Confederations Cup in Japan, which included a memorable 0-0 draw against Brazil. He also served as Canada's captain at three Concacaf Gold Cups from 2000 to 2003. He won Canada Soccer Player of the Year honours in 2002.

GOALKEEPER

PAUL DOLAN

Born: 1966-04-16, Ottawa, ON, CAN. Grew up in Port Moody, BC, CAN. Height 191 cm. Dominant right foot.

1 FIFA World Cup: Group phase at Mexico 1986
1 Concacaf title: 1985 Concacaf Championship
4 cycles FWC Qualifiers: 1985, 1988, 1992-93, 1996-97
1st #CANMNT "A": 1984-10-30 at Nicosia, CYP (v. CYP)
1st Clean Sheet: 1984-10-30 at Nicosia, CYP (v. CYP)

CANADA SOCCER HALL OF FAME

Paul Dolan was Canada's record holder with 19 international clean sheets and 58 international matches as a goalkeeper. He represented Canada in four cycles of FIFA World Cup Qualifiers and famously was in goal for Canada's opening match at the 1986 FIFA World Cup, a narrow 1-0 defeat to the European champions from France. He helped Canada win the 1985 Concacaf Championship and 1990 Three Nations Cup.

After representing Canada at the 1984 Concacaf Youth Championship, he made his international debut at the 1984 Great Wall Championship and made his "A" debut in a 0-0 draw at Nicosia in a friendly against Cyprus.

He was a two-time CSL Championship winner with the Vancouver 86ers and three-time CSL All-Star Team goalkeeper. From the CSL, he continued with the 86ers in the APSL/ A-League where he was named to the All-Star Team and won the 1993 regular-season title.

Dolan played with the Edmonton Brick Men in 1986, then moved to England where he joined Notts County FC. He played the 1987-88 indoor season with the Tacoma Stars.

CANADA RECORDS

INT'L RECORDS	MP	MS	MIN	CS	
1984 CANADA	3	3	225	1	CS
1985 CANADA	14	14	1080	7	CS
1986 CANADA	12	12	1080	5	CS
1988 CANADA	3	3	225	1	CS
1989 CANADA	1	1	90	0	CS
1990 CANADA	0	0	0	0	CS
1991 CANADA	3	3	270	0	CS
1992 CANADA	8	8	697	2	CS
1993 CANADA	2	1	135	0	CS
1994 CANADA	1	1	90	0	CS
1995 CANADA	5	5	407	1	CS
1996 CANADA	2	1	97	1	CS
1997 CANADA	4	4	360	1	CS
14 SEASONS	**58**	**56**	**4756**	**19**	**CS**
FWC QUALIFIERS	16	15	1357	6	CS
GOLD CUP	2	2	180	0	CS
3 NATIONS CUP	1	1	90	0	CS
FIFA WORLD CUP	**MP**	**MS**	**MIN**	**CS**	
1986 FIFA WC	1	1	90	0	CS

1986 FIFA WORLD CUP • Still just 20 years old at Mexico 1986, Paul Dolan was one of the youngest goalkeepers in FIFA World Cup history when he starred for Canada in their opening match against France at Estadio León. Underdogs against the European champions, Canada held France to just one goal scored in the 79th minute.

6

JIMMY DOUGLAS

MIDFIELDER

Born 1948-10-06, Falkirk, SCO. Grew up in Falkirk, SCO & St. Catharines, ON, CAN. Height 183 cm.

1 Olympic Games: Group phase at Montréal 1976
2 cycles FIFA World Cup Qualifiers: 1972, 1976
1st #CANMNT: 1972-08-20 at St. John's, NL, CAN (v. USA)
1st Goal: 1972-08-29 at Baltimore, MD, USA (v. USA)

 CANADA SOCCER HALL OF FAME

Jimmy Douglas was Canada's captain at both the 1975 Pan American Games in Mexico and 1976 Olympic Games in Canada. Across five years from 1972 to 1976, he made 34 career international appearances, at the time ranked third most all time with the Canadian program. He scored seven international goals, two of which he scored at the Olympic Games in 1976.

Douglas was 29 years old when he made his international debut in 1972 FIFA World Cup Qualifiers, a memorable 3-2 win over the Americans in St. John's at King George V Park. While he scored his first international goal nine days later, he is best remembered for his two goals scored four years later at the 1976 Olympic Games.

Douglas played his club football in Ontario, most notably with his hometown St. Catharines Heidelberg SC in the National League Ontario. In 1974, he split the season between St. Catharines and Toronto Metros SC of the North American Soccer League. He was 25 years old when he made his NASL debut on 5 May 1974.

After the Olympic Games, Douglas played with Hamilton Croatia, Toronto First Portuguese and later St. Catharines Roma. He helped St. Catharines finish in fourth place at Canada Soccer's 1978 National Championships.

In 1973, Douglas won the Jimmy Joy Memorial Trophy as the City of St. Catharines' most outstanding athlete.

CANADA RECORDS

INT'L RECORDS	MP	MS	MIN	G	A
1972 CANADA	4	3	-	1	
1973 CANADA	8	6	632	1	2
1974 CANADA	5	5	435		
1975 CANADA	8	8	-	1	3
1976 CANADA	9	9	-	4	
5 SEASONS	**34**	**31**	**n/a**	**7**	**5**
FWC QUALIFIERS	7	6	-	1	

OLYMPIC GAMES	MP	MS	MIN	G	A
1976 OLYMPIC	2	2	180	2	

1976 OLYMPIC GAMES • Captain Jimmy Douglas scored both Canada goals at the 1976 Olympic Football Tournament in Montréal and Toronto. He scored his first goal in the 2-1 loss to the Soviet Union and his second goal in the 3-1 loss to Korea DPR. He scored both of his goals on rebounds.

MIDFIELDER

TERRY DUNFIELD

Born: 1982-02-20, Vancouver, BC, CAN. Height 178 cm. Dominant right foot.

1 cycle FIFA World Cup Qualifiers: 2011-12
1st #CANMNT: 2010-05-29 at Mérida, VEN (v. VEN)
1st Goal: 2011-06-01 at Toronto, ON, CAN (v. ECU)

CANADA HIGHLIGHTS

Terry Dunfield wore the captain's armband at both the youth and international "A" level with Canada. He made 14 career appearances with the Men's National Team and featured in both the 2011 Concacaf Gold Cup and 2011-12 FIFA World Cup Qualifiers. He captained Canada at the 2001 FIFA World Youth Championship.

While Dunfield got his first call up to the Men's National Team in 2004, it wasn't until 2010 that he made his debut at age 28 in a 1-1 away draw at Venezuela. In 2013, he wore the captain's armband in a loss to Denmark in Tucson, Arizona.

CLUB HIGHLIGHTS

Dunfield was just 19 years old when he made his Premier League debut with Manchester City FC in England. He was just the third Canadian to feature in the league. Dunfield made his debut on 19 May on the last day of the 2000-01 season, then just a few days later was in uniform with Canada's U-20 side in preparation for the FIFA World Youth Championship. He was named the club's Most Promising Player by City fans.

From Manchester City FC, Dunfield went to Bury FC, Macclesfield Town FC and then Shrewsbury Town FC. He missed more than two seasons recovering from a knee injury he suffered in January 2005.

He joined his hometown Vancouver Whitecaps in 2010 and followed them into the MLS in 2011. He then joined Toronto FC where he reached the 2011-12 Concacaf Champions League Semifinals and won the 2012 Canadian Championship. He co-led all Canadians with 30 MLS appearances in 2012.

CANADA RECORDS

"A" RECORDS	MP	MS	MIN	G	A
2004 CANADA	0	0	0		
2010 CANADA	2	2	153		
2011 CANADA	7	6	531	1g	
2012 CANADA	1	1	77		
2013 CANADA	4	2	172		
10 SEASONS	**14**	**11**	**933**	**1g**	
FWC QUALIFIERS	3	2	225		
GOLD CUP	3	3	261		

1st INTERNATIONAL GOAL • Terry Dunfield scored his first international goal in Canada's 2-2 home draw with Ecuador at Toronto's BMO Field on 1 June 2011. He scored the opening goal midway through the first half with a right-footed blast from distance. It was Canada's first of 22 matches undefeated in Toronto through 27 June 2023.

5

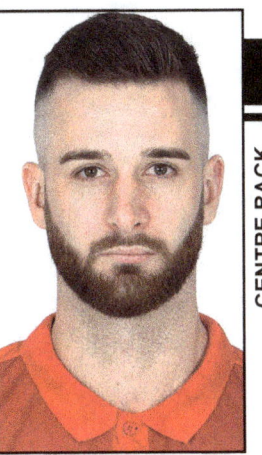

CENTRE BACK

DAVID EDGAR

Born: 1987-05-19, Kitchener, ON, CAN. Height 192 cm. Dominant right foot.

3 cycles FIFA World Cup Qualifiers: 2008, 2011-12, 2015-16
1st #CANMNT: 2011-02-09 at Larissa, GRE (v. GRE)
1st Goal: 2012-10-12 at Toronto, ON, CAN (v. CUB)

CANADA HIGHLIGHTS

David Edgar wore the captain's armband with Canada's youth teams and Men's National Team. He made 42 career international "A" appearances from 2007 to 2019, including three cycles of FIFA World Cup Qualifiers and two editions of the Concacaf Gold Cup. He made five starts as Canada's captain, scored four goals and two assists, and finished as high as third in Player of the Year voting in 2014.

Edgar represented Canada at three FIFA youth tournaments and he earned his first Men's National Team call up just over a month after he featured in every Canada minute at the 2007 FIFA U-20 World Cup in Canada. He was Canada Soccer's U-20 Player of the Year in 2006 and the U-20 runner up in 2007.

CLUB HIGHLIGHTS

Edgar was just 19 years old when he made his Premier League debut with Newcastle United FC on 26 December 2006. He scored his first Premier League goal less than a week later in a 2-2 draw with Manchester United FC on 1 January 2007. In all, he played 10 seasons in England, including three-plus seasons in the Premier League and five-plus seasons in the Championship.

In Canada, he was a two-time North Star Shield winner with Forge FC Hamilton (2019 and 2020). He reached the Concacaf Champions League Semifinals with Vancouver Whitecaps FC in 2016-17.

CANADA RECORDS

"A" RECORDS	MP	MS	MIN	G	A
2007 CANADA	0	0	0		
2008 CANADA	0	0	0		
2010 CANADA	0	0	0		
2011 CANADA	7	5	487		
2012 CANADA	8	8	697	1g	2a
2013 CANADA	7	7	626		
2014 CANADA	4	4	360	1g	
2015 CANADA	9	8	739		
2016 CANADA	6	5	375	2g	
2018 CANADA	1	0	31		
2019 CANADA	0	0	0		
13 SEASONS	**42**	**37**	**3315**	**4g**	**2a**
FWC QUALIFIERS	*17*	*15*	*1354*		*2a*
GOLD CUP	*6*	*6*	*540*		

1st INTERNATIONAL GOAL • David Edgar scored his first international goal in 2012 FIFA World Cup Qualifiers at BMO Field in Toronto, in fact earning Player of the Match honours in the 3-0 win over Cuba. He later scored international goals against Jamaica (2014), Uzbekistan (2016), and El Salvador (2016).

MIDFIELDER

STEPHEN EUSTÁQUIO

Born: 1996-12-21, Leamington, ON, CAN. Grew up in Leamington, ON, CAN & Nazaré, POR. Height 178 cm. Dominant right foot.

1 FIFA World Cup: Group phase at Qatar 2022
1 Concacaf medal: Silver in 2022-23 CNL
1st place FIFA World Cup Qualifiers in 2021-22
1st #CANMNT: 2019-11-15 at Orlando, FL, USA (v. USA)
1st Goal: 2021-07-11 at Kansas City, KS, USA (v. MTQ)

CANADA HIGHLIGHTS

Stephen Eustáquio was one of Canada's leading players at the 2022 FIFA World Cup in Qatar before he suffered an injury. Since 2021, he already helped Canada reach the Semifinals at the Concacaf Gold Cup, finish in first place in the Concacaf Final Round of FIFA World Cup Qualifiers, and won a Silver Medal in Concacaf Nations League. Through December 2023, he has made 34 international "A" appearances, scored three goals and recorded four assists. He was Canada Soccer's Player of the Year in 2023.

After missing more than half a year recovering from a knee injury, Eustáquio made his international debut in November 2019 in Concacaf Nations League.

After the pandemic, he got his first start with Canada in a 5-1 win over Bermuda on 25 March 2021 in FIFA World Cup Qualifiers. That summer, he earned Player of the Match honours for the first time in a 1-0 away win over Haiti in FIFA World Cup Qualifiers and then scored his first international goal in a 4-1 win over Martinique at the Concacaf Gold Cup.

FC PORTO

Since joining FC Porto, Eustáquio has won the 2021-22 Primeira Liga, the 2022 Taça de Portugal, the 2022 Supertaça, and the 2023 Taça da Liga Portuguesa. He also reached the last 16 of 2022-23 UEFA Champions League and scored his first two goals in Europe's top competition.

Before joining FC Porto, he was FC Paços de Ferreira's club MVP in 2020-21.

CANADA RECORDS

"A" RECORDS	MP	MS	MIN	G	A
2019 CANADA	1	0	28		
2020 CANADA	0	0	0		
2021 CANADA	17	15	1344	3g	2a
2022 CANADA	10	10	800		1a
2023 CANADA	6	6	490		1a
UNTIL DEC.2023	34	31	2662	3g	4a
FWC QUALIFIERS	17	15	1330	2g	2a
GOLD CUP	4	4	344	3g	1a
NATIONS LEAGUE	9	8	698		1a

FIFA WORLD CUP	MP	MS	MIN
2022 FIFA WC	2	2	126

2022 FIFA WORLD CUP • Midfielder Stephen Eustáquio made two Canada appearances at the FIFA World Cup in Qatar before he was ruled out through injury. Through 126 minutes, he completed 92.6% of his passes (87 of 94) and ranked first on Canada with an average 20.7 line breaks per 90 minutes played.

2

CENTRE BACK

PAUL FENWICK

Born: 1969-08-25, London, ENG. Grew up in St. Catharines, ON, CAN. Height 187 cm. Dominant right foot.

1 FIFA Confederations Cup: Group phase in 2001
1 Concacaf title: 2000 Concacaf Gold Cup
3 cycles FIFA World Cup Qualifiers: 1993 ,1997, 2000
1st #CANMNT: 1994-06-12 at Toronto, ON, CAN (vs. NED)

CANADA HIGHLIGHTS

Paul Fenwick won the 2000 Concacaf Gold Cup after he helped Canada post back-to-back clean sheets against Trinidad and Tobago and Colombia. That season, he played in a career-high 13 international "A" matches and even wore the captain's armband for a FIFA World Cup Qualifiers match in Winnipeg.

After representing Canada at the Concacaf Youth Championship and then Concacaf Olympic Qualifiers, he made his international "A" debut on 12 June 1994 against Netherlands at Toronto's Varsity Stadium. With the Men's National Team, he helped Canada reach FIFA's intercontinental playoff in 1993 and the Concacaf Final Round in 1997.

CLUB HIGHLIGHTS

Fenwick played his football in Canada, England and Scotland. He moved to the U.K. in 1992 and spent more than a decade overseas, notably joining Scottish Premier League side Hibernian FC where he made appearances in the UEFA Cup.

Fenwick won the 1992 Canadian Soccer League Championship with the Winnipeg Fury before he moved to Europe. He played three seasons in the league and also played with the Kitchener Spirit, Toronto Blizzard and Hamilton Steelers. He was just 20 years old when he made his pro debut on 3 June 1990 with Kitchener.

CANADA RECORDS

"A" RECORDS		MP	MS	MIN
1993	CANADA	0	0	0
1994	CANADA	1	0	25
1995	CANADA	0	0	0
1996	CANADA	2	2	135
1997	CANADA	1	0	7
1999	CANADA	4	4	360
2000	CANADA	13	12	1050
2001	CANADA	3	3	170
2002	CANADA	2	2	153
2003	CANADA	7	5	468
11 SEASONS		**33**	**28**	**2368**
FWC QUALIFIERS		7	6	500
GOLD CUP		6	5	422

CONFEDERATIONS		MP	MS	MIN
2001	FIFA CC	INJ	-	

2001 FIFA CONFEDERATIONS CUP • After he helped Canada qualify for the FIFA Confederations Cup and win the Concacaf Gold Cup in 2000, Paul Fenwick missed the tournament in 2001 through injury. He was selected to the squad, but unable to feature because of a hamstring injury

CENTRE BACK

CARL FLETCHER

13

Born: 1971-12-26, Plymouth, MSR. Grew up in Scarborough, ON, CAN. Height 178 cm. Dominant right foot.

1 FIFA Confederations Cup: Group phase in 2001
3 cycles FIFA World Cup Qualifiers: 1992, 1996-97, 2000
1st #CANMNT "A": 1991-07-03 at Los Angeles, CA, CAN (v. JAM)
1st Goal: 1997-11-16 at San José, CRC (v. CRC)

CANADA HIGHLIGHTS

Carl Fletcher featured in all three matches at the FIFA Confederations Cup, including the last 20-plus minutes of a 0-0 draw with Brazil. Across 13 years, he took part in the Concacaf Final Round of 1997 FIFA World Cup Qualifiers and helped Canada qualify for the 2000 Concacaf Gold Cup through the qualifiers in October 1999, but he ultimately missed the Concacaf Gold Cup through injury.

Fletcher was 19 years old when he made his international "A" debut at the inaugural Concacaf Gold Cup in 1991. He scored his first goal in 1997 FIFA World Cup Qualifiers at Costa Rica and his second goal two years later in Gold Cup Qualifying against El Salvador. As a youth player, he represented Canada at their home FIFA U-16 World Tournament in 1987.

CLUB HIGHLIGHTS

Fletcher played 15 pro seasons in Canada and the United States, notably winning back-to-back A-League regular season titles with the Impact de Montréal in 1996 and 1997 and then the 2001 USL A-League Championship with the Rochester Rhinos.

Fletcher played four years with Toronto in the Canadian League where he was an all-star in 1992. He was 17 years old when he made his pro debut on 28 May 1989.

CANADA RECORDS

"A" RECORDS	MP	MS	MIN	G	A
1991 CANADA	1	1	38		
1992 CANADA	1	0	28		
1994 CANADA	0	0	0		
1995 CANADA	1	1	90		
1996 CANADA	3	2	225		
1997 CANADA	3	1	156	1g	
1998 CANADA	1	1	90		
1999 CANADA	7	5	455	1g	
2000 CANADA	9	8	745		
2001 CANADA	6	4	426		
2002 CANADA	4	4	287		
2003 CANADA	4	3	244		
13 SEASONS	**40**	**30**	**2784**	**2g**	
FWC QUALIFIERS	7	4	498	1g	
GOLD CUP	6	5	400		

CONFEDERATIONS	MP	MS	MIN
2001 FIFA CC	3	2	201

CONCACAF GOLD CUP QUALIFYING • Carl Fletcher scored Canada's 2-1 match winner when they beat El Salvador in Concacaf Gold Cup Qualifiers in 1999. Two days later in the group finale, he was part of the build up on Canada's opening goal when they beat Haiti 2-1 to officially qualify for the 2000 Concacaf Gold Cup.

CRAIG FOREST

Born: 1967-09-20, Coquitlam, BC, CAN.   Height 196 cm. Dominant right foot.

1 FIFA Confederations Cup: Group phase in 2001
1 Concacaf title: 2000 Concacaf Gold Cup
2 cycles FIFA World Cup Qualifiers: 1992-93, 1996-97
1st #CANMNT: 1988-05-25 at Toronto, ON, CAN (v. CHI)
1st Clean Sheet: 1988-05-25 at Toronto, ON, CAN (v. CHI)

CANADA SOCCER HALL OF FAME

Craig Forrest was the tournament MVP when Canada won the 2000 Concacaf Gold Cup after they qualified for the FIFA Confederations Cup. Across 14 years, he was Canada's record holder with 56 international "A" goalkeeper appearances and 19 clean sheets. He was also Canada Soccer's Player of the Year in 1994 and 2000.

A year after the 1987 FIFA World Youth Championship, he posted back-to-back clean sheets in his first two "A" matches when Canada won the 1988 Sir Stanley Matthews Cup. At the 2000 Concacaf Gold Cup, he posted back-to-back clean sheets to beat Trinidad and Tobago (including a penalty save) and Colombia. At the 2001 FIFA Confederations Cup, he earned Player of the Match honours in a 0-0 draw with Brazil at Kashima Stadium in Japan.

Forrest played in the Premier League with Ipswich Town FC, Chelsea FC and West Ham United FC. He was the Ipswich Town FC Player of the Year in 1994-95 when he made a career-high 36 appearances in the Premier League. In 1991-92, he helped Ipswich Town win the Second Division and earn promotion to the first Premier League season in 1992-93.

CANADA RECORDS

"A" RECORDS		MP	MS	MIN	CS	
1988	CANADA	4	4	390	2	CS
1989	CANADA	2	2	180	0	CS
1990	CANADA	1	1	90	0	CS
1991	CANADA	1	1	28	0	CS
1992	CANADA	3	3	270	1	CS
1993	CANADA	11	11	1020	2	CS
1994	CANADA	4	4	360	0	CS
1995	CANADA	3	3	270	0	CS
1996	CANADA	8	8	713	4	CS
1997	CANADA	7	7	630	2	CS
1999	CANADA	1	1	90	0	CS
2000	CANADA	7	7	614	5	CS
2001	CANADA	4	4	360	2	CS
14 SEASONS		**56**	**56**	**5015**	**18**	**CS**
FWC QUALIFIERS		*21*	*21*	*1913*	*7*	*CS*
GOLD CUP		*10*	*10*	*840*	*3*	*CS*
3 NATIONS CUP		*2*	*2*	*180*	*1*	*CS*

CONFEDERATIONS		MP	MS	MIN	CS	
2001	FIFA CC	3	3	270	1	CS

PLAYER OF THE YEAR • After the award was introduced in 1993, Craig Forrest was a two-time Canada Soccer Player of the Year (1994, 2001) and two-time runner up (1993, 1996). In the Premier League, he posted a career-best 10 clean sheets in 1993-94 and won Ipswich Town FC Player of the Year honours in 1994-95.

FORWARD

ROB FRIEND

Born: 1981-01-23, Rosetown, SK, CAN. Grew up in Kelowna, BC, CAN. Height 196 cm. Dominant right foot.

1 cycle FIFA World Cup Qualifiers: 2008
1st #CANMNT: 2003-01-18 at Ft Lauderdale, FL, USA (v. USA)
1st Goal: 2006-09-04 at Montréal, QC, CAN (v. JAM)

CANADA HIGHLIGHTS

Rob Friend made 32 career international "A" appearances from 2003 to 2012, including one cycle of FIFA World Cup Qualifiers and two editions of the Concacaf Gold Cup. He was part of the Canada squad that reached the Concacaf Gold Cup Semifinals in 2007, then started up front in both a 2008 friendly against Brazil and 2010 friendly against Argentina. He led all Canadians with 387 minutes played in 2006.

After representing Canada at the 2001 FIFA World Youth Championship, Friend scored 12 goals with the U-23 squad across the Jeux de la Francophonie in 2001 and Concacaf Olympic Qualifiers in 2003-04. He scored six goals in one match against US Virgin Islands.

CLUB HIGHLIGHTS

Friend helped three clubs win promotion to the Bundesliga in a five-year span: Borussia Mönchengladbach in 2007-08; Hertha HSC in 2010-11; and Eintracht Frankfurt in 2011-12. He was the second-best marksman in 2007-08 2.Bundesliga with 18 goals, the most ever by a Canadian in Germany's first or second division.

Friend played his youth soccer in British Columbia before he moved to Europe where he played in Norway, Netherlands and Germany. He won the Norway Cup with Molde FK in 2005 and featured in the UEFA Cup with sc Heerenveen in 2006-07.

Friend joined the Los Angeles Galaxy in 2014 and won the MLS Cup.

CANADA RECORDS

"A" RECORDS	MP	MS	MIN	G	A
2003 CANADA	3	0	44		
2004 CANADA	1	0	28		
2006 CANADA	5	4	387	1g	
2007 CANADA	5	3	325		1a
2008 CANADA	8	5	412	1g	
2009 CANADA	2	1	86		
2010 CANADA	3	3	224		1a
2011 CANADA	5	1	199		
2012 CANADA	0	0	0		
10 SEASONS	**32**	**17**	**1705**	**2g**	**2a**
FWC QUALIFIERS	5	3	232		
GOLD CUP	4	2	215		

● ● ●

1st INTERNATIONAL GOAL • Rob Friend scored his first international "A" goal in Head Coach Stephen Hart's first match in charge with Canada in 2006, a 1-0 home win over Jamaica. Two years later, Friend scored a memorable goal in a 3-2 loss to Brazil in front of 47,052 spectators in Seattle.

10

ALI GERBA

FORWARD

Born: 1981-04-09, Yaoundé, CMR. Grew up in Montréal, QC, CAN. Height 183 cm. Dominant right foot.

1 cycle FIFA World Cup Qualifiers: 2008
1st #CANMNT: 2005-07-02 at Burnaby, BC, CAN (v. HON)
1st Goal: 2005-07-12 at Foxborough, MA, USA (v. CUB)

CANADA HIGHLIGHTS

Ali Gerba was a Canada record holder with six international goals scored in 2008, the first of two seasons in which he led Canada in goals scored. He scored 15 career goals in just 31 international matches from 2005 to 2011, including matches across one cycle of FIFA World Cup Qualifiers and four editions of the Concacaf Gold Cup. He reached the Concacaf Gold Cup Semifinals in 2007.

A Canada youth player from 1999 to 2001, he made his international "A" debut less than a week before the 2005 Concacaf Gold Cup, then scored his first goal against Cuba in Canada's third group match.

CLUB HIGHLIGHTS

Gerba played his club football in Canada, USA, Sweden, Norway, Denmark, Germany and England. In 2007-08, he helped FC Ingolstadt 04 win promotion to the 2.Bundesliga. In 2008-09, he helped Milton Keynes Dons FC finish third in League One before they were eliminated in the promotion playoffs. He scored 10 goals in 24 matches that season in League One.

In Canada, Gerba played with the Montréal Impact, Toronto Lynx and Toronto FC. He scored six times as an A-League rookie in 2000 with Montréal, then got picked 18th overall in the 2001 MLS SuperDraft by the Miami Fusion. In 2004 with the Toronto Lynx, he won team MVP honours after he scored 15 goals in 25 matches.

From 2008 to 2010, Gerba won Soccer Québec Player of the Year honours in three successive years.

CANADA RECORDS

"A" RECORDS	MP	MS	MIN	G	A
2005 CANADA	5	3	278	1g	
2006 CANADA	2	1	80		
2007 CANADA	7	5	376	4g	1a
2008 CANADA	9	5	504	6g	1a
2009 CANADA	5	4	361	4g	
2010 CANADA	1	1	90		
2011 CANADA	2	1	88		
7 SEASONS	*31*	*20*	*1777*	*15g*	*2a*
FWC QUALIFIERS	*7*	*4*	*414*	*6g*	*1a*
GOLD CUP	*13*	*9*	*755*	*6g*	*1a*

FIFA WORLD CUP QUALIFIERS • Ali Gerba was Canada's top goalscorer across FIFA World Cup Qualifiers in 2008 when he scored six goals in seven matches, including goals both away and back home against Mexico. He finished third that year in voting for Player of the Year honours.

MIDFIELDER

GERRY GRAY

Born: 1961-01-20, Glasgow, SCO. Grew up in Toronto, ON, CAN. Height 170 cm. Dominant right foot.

1 FIFA World Cup: Group phase at Mexico 1986
1 Olympic Games: Quarterfinals at Los Angeles 1984
2 cycles FIFA World Cup Qualifiers: 1980-81, 1988
1st #CANMNT: 1979-04-01 at Devonshire Parish, BER (v. BER)
1st Goal: 1979-04-08 at Hamilton, BER (v. MEX)

CANADA SOCCER HALL OF FAME

Gerry Gray made 54 international appearances for Canada, ranked sixth all-time after his last international match on 31 March 1991 at the North American Nations Cup. Across 13 years, Gray notably represented Canada at the 1984 Olympic Games at Los Angeles as well as the 1986 FIFA World Cup in Mexico. From 1980 to 1983, he played in a career-high 18 consecutive "A" matches and was part of the Canada squad that came within a goal of qualifying for the 1982 FIFA World Cup in Spain.

Gray was just 18 years old when he made his international debut in Pan American Games Qualifiers on 1 April 1979 in Bermuda. He scored his first two goals a week later against Mexico, played in the 1979 FIFA World Youth Championship in August, then made his international "A" debut a year later on 15 September 1980 in Vancouver. Two months later, he scored a famous 1-1 equaliser against Mexico at Estadio Azteca in front of 90,000 fans during FIFA World Cup Qualifiers.

Gray was a 1984 NASL Championship winner with the Chicago Sting after five seasons in the North American League. He started his career with the Vancouver Whitecaps before playing with the CS Manic de Montréal, New York Cosmos and Chicago. Later in the Canadian Soccer League, he reached the 1989 CSL Final with the Hamilton Steelers.

CANADA RECORDS

INT'L RECORDS	MP	MS	MIN	G	A
1979 CANADA	4	4	360	2g	2a
1980 CANADA	10	10	-	2g	3a
1981 CANADA	9	9	-	1g	1a
1983 CANADA	6	6	512	1g	1a
1984 CANADA	7	7	660	2g	
1986 CANADA	6	6	508	1g	
1988 CANADA	9	7	730		1a
1989 CANADA	1	1	90		
1991 CANADA	2	2	180		
13 SEASONS	54	52	n/a	9g	8a
FWC QUALIFIERS	11	11	945	1g	3a
3 NATIONS CUP	2	2	180		

FIFA / OLYMPIC	MP	MS	MIN
1984 OLYMPIC	4	4	390
1986 FIFA WC	2	2	159

1984 OLYMPIC GAMES • Gerry Gray played in every Canada minute at the 1984 Olympic Football Tournament as they reached the Quarterfinals for the first time. They were eliminated in the knockout phase by the Silver Medal winners Brazil. In the opening match of the group phase, Gray scored Canada's opening goal in a 1-1 draw with Iraq.

4

ANDRÉ HAINAULT

CENTRE BACK

Born: 1986-06-17, Montréal, QC, CAN. Grew up in Hudson, QC, CAN. Height 184 cm. Dominant right foot.

3 cycles FIFA World Cup Qualifiers: 2008, 2011-12, 2016
1st #CANMNT: 2006-11-15 at Székesfehérvár, HUN (v. HUN)
1st Goal: 2008-10-11 at San Pedro Sula, HON (v. HON)

CANADA HIGHLIGHTS

André Hainault made 44 career international "A" appearances over 11 years, including three cycles of FIFA World Cup Qualifiers and four editions of the Concacaf Gold Cup. He played in every Canada minute at the 2007 Concacaf Gold Cup when they reached the Semifinals.

Hainault wore the captain's armband at the 2003 Concacaf Under-17 Championship and 2008 Concacaf Olympic Qualifiers, helping the U-23 squad come within a victory of reaching the Beijing Olympic Games. He featured in every Canada minute at the 2005 FIFA World Youth Championship in the Netherlands.

He was 20 years old when he made his international "A" debut in a narrow 1-0 loss to Hungary in 2006.

CLUB HIGHLIGHTS

Hainault was a two-time MLS Cup finalist with the Houston Dynamo where he spent four seasons in the United States. In 2011, he won Houston Defender of the Year honours and set a record for most minutes by a Canadian in an MLS season.

As a teenager, Hainault was part of the Montréal Impact side that won the 2005 Commissioner's Cup as the regular season champions.

In Europe, Hainault played in the Czech Republic, Scotland and Germany. He played two seasons in Germany's 2.Bundesliga with VfR Aalen.

CANADA RECORDS

"A" RECORDS	MP	MS	MIN	G	A
2006 CANADA	1	1	90		
2007 CANADA	8	8	704		
2008 CANADA	5	4	405	1g	
2009 CANADA	1	1	90		
2010 CANADA	2	2	180		
2011 CANADA	7	6	591	1g	
2012 CANADA	8	8	720		
2013 CANADA	5	4	396		
2014 CANADA	4	4	315		1a
2015 CANADA	3	1	123		
2016 CANADA	0	0	0		
11 SEASONS	**44**	**39**	**3614**	**2g**	**1a**
FWC QUALIFIERS	*11*	*11*	*990*	*1g*	
GOLD CUP	*11*	*9*	*843*		

1st INTERNATIONAL GOAL • André Hainault scored his first goal in a FIFA World Cup Qualifiers 3-1 away loss to Honduras in San Pedro Sula. The goal came off his right knee after a Kevin McKenna header hit the crossbar (from an Iain Hume free kick). Hainault later scored his second international goal in a 2011 frienldy against Belarus.

LEFT BACK / CB

RICHARD HASTINGS

3

Born: 1977-05-18, Prince George, BC, CAN. Grew up in Middlesbrough, ENG & Inverness, SCO. Height 183 cm. Dominant left foot.

1 FIFA Confederations Cup: Group phase in 2001
1 Concacaf title: 2000 Concacaf Gold Cup
2 cycles FIFA World Cup Qualifiers: 2000, 2008
1st #CANMNT: 1998-05-18 at Toronto, ON, CAN (v. MKD)
1st Goal: 2000-02-20 at San Diego, CA, USA (v. MEX)

CANADA SOCCER HALL OF FAME

Richard Hastings became Canada's golden goal hero when he scored the 2-1 match winner in the 2000 Concacaf Gold Cup Quarterfinals against Mexico. He helped Canada qualify for the FIFA Confederations Cup and win the Concacaf Gold Cup.

It was his first of five Concacaf Gold Cups, which included a third-place finish in 2002 and a Semifinals finish in 2007. He was named a Concacaf Gold Cup All-Star in 2007.

Hastings helped Canada win the Concacaf Youth Championship in 1996 and then feature at the 1997 FIFA World Youth Championship. He was just 20 years old when he made his international debut on 18 May 1998 against Macedonia, with his corner kick headed home by Niall Thompson for the 1-0 win at Toronto's Varsity Stadium.

Hastings was a club hero at Inverness Caledonian Thistle FC where he won the Scottish Third Division (1996-97) and twice won promotion to a higher division (in 1996-97 to the Second Division; in 1998-99 to the First Division). On 8 February 2000, he was part of the squad that beat Celtic FC in the Scottish Cup.

CANADA RECORDS

"A" RECORDS	MP	MS	MIN	G	A
1998 CANADA	1	1	63		1a
1999 CANADA	2	2	171		
2000 CANADA	14	12	1078	1g	
2001 CANADA	3	2	225		
2002 CANADA	7	7	690		
2003 CANADA	9	9	795		
2004 CANADA	0	0	0		
2007 CANADA	8	8	720		
2008 CANADA	9	8	688		
2009 CANADA	4	3	315		
2010 CANADA	2	2	171		
13 SEASONS	**59**	**54**	**4916**	**1g**	**1a**
FWC QUALIFIERS	11	9	803		
GOLD CUP	18	17	1608	1g	

CONFEDERATIONS	MP	MS	MIN
2001 FIFA CC	0	0	0

CONCACAF GOLD CUP • Richard Hastings was the Concacaf Gold Cup's Top Rookie in 2000 when Canada captured their second confederation title in men's football. After his famous goal in the Quarterfinals, he helped Canada post back-to-back clean sheets against Trinidad and Tobago as well as Colombia to lift the Concacaf Gold Cup.

15

DONEIL HENRY

CENTRE BACK

Born: 1993-04-20, North York, ON, CAN. Grew up in Brampton, ON, CAN. Height 173 cm. Dominant right foot.

Missed FIFA World Cup in 2022 through injury
1st place FIFA World Cup Qualifiers in 2021-22
1st #CANMNT: 2012-08-15 at Lauderhill, FL, USA (v. TRI)
1st Goal: 2019-09-07 at Toronto, ON, CAN (v. CUB)

CANADA HIGHLIGHTS

Doneil Henry helped Canada qualify for the 2022 FIFA World Cup and win the Concacaf Final Round of FIFA World Cup Qualifiers, but he only missed the final competition in Qatar through injury. Through December 2023, he has already made 44 career Canada appearances including two cycles of FIFA World Cup Qualifiers and three editions of the Concacaf Gold Cup. He helped Canada reach the Concacaf Gold Cup Semifinals in 2021.

At the U-23 level in 2012, Henry helped Canada climb to within a victory of the London 2012 Olympic Games by reaching the Semifinals at the Concacaf Olympic Qualifiers. After he made his international "A" debut in August, he wore the captain's armband at the Concacaf Under-20 Championship in 2013.

CLUB HIGHLIGHTS

Henry has played continental football in Concacaf, Europe and Asia. A three-time Canadian Championship winner with Toronto FC, he suited up for Premier League side West Ham United FC and also featured in the Championship with the Blackburn Rovers. In 2020, he became the first Canadian to feature in the K League with the Suwon Samsung Bluewings.

In 2018, Henry was named the Vancouver Whitecaps FC Humanitarian of the Year.

CANADA RECORDS

"A" RECORDS		MP	MS	MIN	G	A
2012	CANADA	1	1	45		
2013	CANADA	10	9	833		
2014	CANADA	3	3	270		
2016	CANADA	8	7	675		
2018	CANADA	2	2	180		
2019	CANADA	7	7	502	1g	
2020	CANADA	0	0	0		
2021	CANADA	10	7	608		
2022	CANADA	3	2	183		
11 SEASONS		**44**	**38**	**3296**	**1g**	
FWC QUALIFIERS		12	11	921		
GOLD CUP		10	8	710		
NATIONS LEAGUE		4	3	202	1g	

FIFA WORLD CUP	MP	MS	MIN
2022 FIFA WC	INJ	-	-

FIFA WORLD CUP QUALIFIERS • Doneil Henry was on the pitch for six of Canada's 12 clean sheets in FIFA World Cup Qualifiers, including the 0-0 away draw at Jamaica when he wore the captain's armband and the historic 4-0 home win over Jamaica when Canada qualified for the men's FIFA World Cup for the first time in 36 years.

GOALKEEPER

LARS HIRSCHFELD

Born: 1978-10-17, Edmonton, AB, CAN. Height 190 cm. Dominant right foot.

3 cycles FIFA World Cup Qualifiers: 2004, 2008, 2011-12
1st #CANMNT: 2000-01-11 at Devonshire Parish, BER (v. BER)
1st Clean Sheet: 2002-01-18 at Miami, FL, USA (v. HAI)

CANADA HIGHLIGHTS

Lars Hirschfeld was the Best Goalkeeper at the 2002 Concacaf Gold Cup when Canada finished in third place at the biennial tournament. It was his first of five Concacaf Gold Cups across a 17-year international career that also included three cycles of FIFA World Cup Qualifiers.

After finishing in fourth place at the 1999 Pan American Games in Winnipeg, Hirschfeld made his "A" debut on 11 January 2000 against Bermuda as a substitute. While he wasn't selected for the Concacaf Gold Cup that year, he was the nation's first goalkeeper in 2002 when he played every minute and posted clean sheets against Haiti (2-0) and USA (0-0).

CLUB HIGHLIGHTS

Hirschfeld had two successful stints in Norway: the first in which he won the 2006 Tippeligaen and qualified for UEFA Champions League; the second in which he helped his club finish second in the 2010 standings and qualified for UEFA Europa League. He was the Rosenborg BK Player of the Year in 2006 and the Vålerenga IF Player of the Year in 2010.

Across his career, he also won Canada Soccer's National Championships in 1997, the Romania Liga 1 in 2007-08 and back-to-back Romanian cups in 2008 and 2009.

CANADA RECORDS

"A" RECORDS	MP	MS	MIN	CS
1999 CANADA	0	0	0	0 CS
2000 CANADA	1	0	18	0 CS
2001 CANADA	1	1	45	0 CS
2002 CANADA	7	7	690	2 CS
2003 CANADA	7	6	540	2 CS
2004 CANADA	1	1	90	1 CS
2005 CANADA	1	1	90	0 CS
2007 CANADA	3	3	270	1 CS
2008 CANADA	6	6	540	0 CS
2009 CANADA	2	2	180	1 CS
2010 CANADA	3	3	270	0 CS
2011 CANADA	6	5	495	4 CS
2012 CANADA	7	7	559	5 CS
2013 CANADA	3	3	225	1 CS
2014 CANADA	0	0	0	0 CS
2015 CANADA	0	0	0	0 CS
17 SEASONS	**48**	**45**	**4012**	**17 CS**
FWC QUALIFIERS	15	15	1324	7 CS
GOLD CUP	8	8	780	3 CS

● ● ●

FIFA WORLD CUP QUALIFIERS • Lars Hirschfeld tied a Canada record when he posted six clean sheets in a single cycle of FIFA World Cup Qualifiers in 2011-12. He tied the mark previously set by Craig Forrest in 1996-97. Across Hirschfeld's career, he posted 17 career clean sheets in 48 international "A" matches.

10

JUNIOR HOILETT

WINGER / FORWARD

Born: 1990-06-05, Brampton, ON, CAN. Height 174 cm. Dominant right foot.

1 FIFA World Cup: Group phase at Qatar 2022
1 Concacaf medal: Silver in 2022-23 CNL
1st place FIFA World Cup Qualifiers in 2021-22
1st #CANMNT: 2015-10-13 at Washington, DC, USA (v. GHA)
1st Goal: 2017-07-20 at Glendale, AZ, USA (v. JAM)

CANADA HIGHLIGHTS

Junior Hoilett is a former Canada record holder for international "A" assists and he ranked second behind Alphonso Davies at the end of 2023. He helped Canada win the 2021-22 Concacaf Final Round of FIFA World Cup Qualifiers, featured in all three Canada matches at the 2022 FIFA World Cup in Qatar, and won a Concacaf Silver Medal at the 2022-23 Nations League Finals.

Hoilett also shares the Canada record for goals scored at the Concacaf Gold Cup and he is the only Canadian to score in four different editions of the competition (six goals from 2017 to 2023). He has helped Canada reach the knockout phase in four consecutive editions, including 2021 when his match winner against Costa Rica pushed Canada into the Semifinals for the first time in 14 years.

ABERDEEN FC

Hoilett has already played 15 seasons in the United Kingdom including six seasons in the Premier League. He helped Queens Park Rangers win promotion from the Championship in 2013-14 and then Cardiff City FC win promotion from the Championship in 2017-18. He was the Cardiff City FC Players' Player Award winner in 2017-18.

He joined Aberdeen FC in 2023-24 after a brief stint with Vancouver Whitecaps FC in 2023.

CANADA RECORDS

"A" RECORDS	MP	MS	MIN	G	A
2015 CANADA	3	3	249		
2016 CANADA	7	6	535		3a
2017 CANADA	7	7	600	1g	1a
2018 CANADA	3	3	251	2g	2a
2019 CANADA	7	5	477	6g	4a
2021 CANADA	12	8	638	4g	4a
2022 CANADA	14	8	746	1g	
2023 CANADA	9	4	363	2g	2a
UNTIL DEC.2023	62	44	3859	16g	16a
FWC QUALIFIERS	19	13	1088	3g	4a
GOLD CUP	16	15	1181	6g	6a
NATIONS LEAGUE	9	2	280	3g	1a

FIFA WORLD CUP	MP	MS	MIN		
2022 FIFA WC	3	2	153		

2022 FIFA WORLD CUP • Junior Hoilett featured in all three Canada matches at the 2022 FIFA World Cup in Qatar, including starts against Belgium and Morocco. In FIFA World Cup Qualifiers, he scored in the historic 4-0 home win over Jamaica on 27 March 2022 when Canada qualified for the men's FIFA World Cup for the first time in 36 years.

MIDFIELDER

LYNDON HOOPER

Born: 1966-05-30, Georgetown, GUY. Grew up in Nepean, ON, CAN. Height 170 cm. Dominant right foot.

3 cycles FIFA World Cup Qualifiers: 1988, 1992-93, 1996-97
1st #CANMNT: 1986-08-25 at Kallang, SIN (v. SIN)
1st Goal: 1986-08-25 at Kallang, SIN (v. MAS "B")

CANADA SOCCER HALL OF FAME

Lyndon Hooper made 78 international appearances for Canada, ranked third all-time after his last match on 1 June 1997 at Edmonton's Commonwealth Stadium. Across 12 years, he took part in three cycles of FIFA World Cup Qualifiers, reaching the intercontinental playoff in 1993 and the Concacaf Final Round in 1997. He also featured in Canada's 1994 historic 1-1 draw with Brazil in front of a Canadian record crowd of 51,936 spectators at Commonwealth Stadium.

After representing Canada at the youth level, he made his Men's National Team debut at age 20 in Singapore just over eight weeks after the 1986 FIFA World Cup. He then featured in Olympic Qualifying in 1987, helped Canada win the 1988 Sir Stanley Matthews Cup in Toronto, and won a Gold Medal at the 1989 Jeux de la Francophonie.

At the club level, Hooper helped the Montréal Impact win the A-League Commissioner's Cup as regular season champions in three successive seasons from 1995 to 1997. In all, he played more than a decade across the Canadian Soccer League and APSL / A-League. He also played overseas in England.

In the Canadian League, he was a three-time CSL All-Star and he reached the CSL Final with Toronto in 1991. He was 21 years old when he made his professional debut on 7 June 1987 with Ottawa.

CANADA RECORDS

"A" RECORDS	MP	MS	MIN	G	A
1986 CANADA	6	6	540	1g	
1987 CANADA	4	3	292		
1988 CANADA	15	14	1315	1g	
1989 CANADA	5	4	390	1g	
1991 CANADA	2	2	180		
1992 CANADA	8	4	-		
1993 CANADA	13	12	1060	1g	
1994 CANADA	5	4	312		
1995 CANADA	7	7	598		
1996 CANADA	9	9	704		1a
1997 CANADA	4	2	175		
12 SEASONS	**78**	**67**	**n/a**	**4g**	**1a**
FWC QUALIFIERS	21	18	1530	1g	
GOLD CUP	5	5	450		1a
3 NATIONS CUP	2	2	180		

FIFA WORLD CUP QUALIFIERS • Lyndon Hooper scored his first competitive goal in the 1993 FIFA World Cup Qualifiers intercontinental playoff, but it was not enough as Australia beat Canada across the home-and-away series. He scored his goal away in Sydney on a shot from distance that slipped through the goalkeeper's hands.

7

IAIN HUME

FORWARD

Born: 1983-10-30, Edinburgh, SCO. Grew up in Brampton, ON, CAN. Height 173 cm. Dominant right foot.

3 cycles FIFA World Cup Qualifiers: 2004, 2008, 2011-12
1st #CANMNT: 2003-02-12 at Tripoli, LBY (v. LBY)
1st Goal: 2005-11-16 at Hesperange, LUX (v. LUX)

CANADA HIGHLIGHTS

Iain Hume represented Canada in three cycles of FIFA World Cup Qualifiers and three editions of the Concacaf Gold Cup. Across 14 years, he made 43 career international appearances, scored six goals, and helped Canada reach the Concacaf Gold Cup Semifinals in 2007.

Hume played at two FIFA World Youth Championships, most notably UAE 2003 when he was named to the tournament's all-star team after Canada reached the Quarterfinals. Hume scored all three Canada goals in that tournament, including the 1-1 equaliser in those Quarterfinals before Spain won 2-1 in extra time.

Hume scored his first Canada goal in 2005 against Luxembourg, but scored his most famous goal in the 2007 Concacaf Semifinals against the Americans.

CLUB HIGHLIGHTS

Hume scored more than 100 goals in England, notably featuring in the Championship with Leicester City FC, Barnsley FC and Preston North End FC. He helped Doncaster Rovers (2012-13) and Fleetwood Town FC (2013-14) earn promotion.

In the Indian Super League, he was the Best Player in 2014 after he led Kerala Blasters to the playoff final. Two years later, he won the Championship in 2016 with Atlético de Kolkata.

CANADA RECORDS

"A" RECORDS	MP	MS	MIN	G	A
2003 CANADA	3	1	130		
2004 CANADA	7	6	455		2a
2005 CANADA	4	2	171	1g	
2006 CANADA	2	1	89		
2007 CANADA	6	2	226	1g	
2008 CANADA	4	0	160		1a
2009 CANADA	2	1	69		
2010 CANADA	1	0	27		
2011 CANADA	4	4	296	3g	1a
2012 CANADA	5	0	88	1g	
2013 CANADA	1	1	45		
2015 CANADA	2	1	78		
2016 CANADA	2	0	39		
14 SEASONS	**43**	**19**	**1873**	**6g**	**4a**
FWC QUALIFIERS	*17*	*9*	*890*	*4g*	*4a*
GOLD CUP	*5*	*0*	*137*	*1g*	

FIFA WORLD CUP QUALIFIERS • Iain Hume was Canada's joint top goalscorer across FIFA World Cup Qualifiers in 2011 and 2012. He scored four goals in eight matches, including wins over Puerto Rico and St. Lucia. He recorded two goals and one assist in Canada's 7-0 win over St. Lucia in October 2011.

MIDFIELDER

ATIBA HUTCHINSON

13

Born: 2003-01-18, North York, ON, CAN. Grew up in Brampton, ON, CAN. Height 185 cm. Dominant right foot.

1 FIFA World Cup: Group phase at Qatar 2022
1 Concacaf medal: Silver in 2022-23 CNL
1st place FIFA World Cup Qualifiers in 2021-22
1st #CANMNT: 2003-01-18 at Ft Lauderdale, FL, USA (v. USA)
1st Goal: 2004-10-09 at San Pedro Sula, HON (v. HON)

CANADA HIGHLIGHTS

Atiba Hutchinson featured in a record 104 appearances with Canada Soccer's Men's National Team across 22 international seasons from 2002 to 2023. He was a six-time Canada Soccer Player of the Year.

He featured in two editions of the FIFA World Youth Championship, including a Quarterfinals finish in 2003 when he was named a tournament all-star. With the Men's National Team, he featured in a record 43 career wins including Canada's 4-0 victory over Jamaica when Canada qualified for the FIFA World Cup.

His most famous goal was the 2-2 equaliser he scored onside in the 2007 Concacaf Gold Cup Semifinals against USA, although it was infamously denied by the referee.

In Europe, he played 16 seasons in UEFA club competitions with FC København, PSV Eindhoven and Beşiktaş JK. He won titles with all three clubs. He was a club legend at Beşiktaş where he played 10 seasons and won three Turkish Süper Lig titles.

CANADA RECORDS

"A" RECORDS	MP	MS	MIN	G	A
2002 CANADA	0	0	0		
2003 CANADA	4	2	208		
2004 CANADA	7	7	578	1	
2005 CANADA	7	7	618	1	
2006 CANADA	4	4	315		
2007 CANADA	9	9	747	1	2
2008 CANADA	9	9	784		
2009 CANADA	7	7	604		1
2010 CANADA	3	2	191	1	1
2011 CANADA	5	5	429		1
2012 CANADA	7	6	559		1
2013 CANADA	3	3	248		
2014 CANADA	4	4	352	1	
2015 CANADA	4	4	360	1	
2016 CANADA	4	4	360		
2017 CANADA	1	1	64		
2018 CANADA	2	2	180	1	
2019 CANADA	4	4	340		1
2021 CANADA	6	4	373	1	
2022 CANADA	11	9	733	1	1
2023 CANADA	3	0	62		
22 SEASONS	**104**	**93**	**8105**	**9**	**8**
FWC QUALIFIERS	*38*	*34*	*3092*	*4*	*2*
GOLD CUP	*18*	*16*	*1467*	*1*	*3*
NATIONS LEAGUE	*5*	*2*	*187*		

FIFA WORLD CUP	MP	MS	MIN	G	A
2022 FIFA WC	3	2	160		

2022 FIFA WORLD CUP • Atiba Hutchinson captained Canada back to the men's FIFA World Cup for the first time in 36 years in 2022. Across three matches in Qatar, he completed 92.7% of his passes (101 completed passes) and he led all Canadians with an average of nine possession regains in defensive actions for every 90 minutes played.

2

ROBERT IARUSCI

Born: 1954-11-08, Toronto, ON, CAN. Height 183 cm. Dominant right foot.

2 cycles FIFA World Cup Qualifiers: 1976-77, 1980-81
1st #CANMNT: 1976-09-24 at Vancouver, BC, CAN (v. USA)
1st Goal: 1980-11-01 at Vancouver, BC, CAN (v. USA)

RIGHT BACK / CB

CANADA SOCCER HALL OF FAME

Robert Iarusci made 31 career international appearances for Canada from 1976 to 1983, including a Men's National Team record 20 consecutive Canada "A" appearances from 1977 to 1983. He represented Canada in back-to-back cycles of FIFA World Cup Qualifiers, helping his nation reach the Concacaf Final Round in 1977 and then captaining the squad to within a goal of qualifying for the 1982 FIFA World Cup in Spain. He wore the captain's armband across the 1980 and 1981 international seasons.

In the 1981 Concacaf Final Round of FIFA World Cup Qualifiers, Iarusci helped Canada post one win, three draws and just one loss to the hosts and group winners Honduras. Canada missed qualification one point back of second-place El Salvador.

Iarusci was a four-time NASL Championship winner, once with Toronto Metros-Croatia and three times with the New York Cosmos. In all, he played nine seasons in the NASL from 1976 to 1984 with Toronto, New York, the Washington Diplomats and San Diego Sockers.

He won playoff titles in 1976, 1977, 1978 and 1982 and finished as a runner up in 1981.

Before turning pro, Iarusci helped Toronto Italia FC win back-to-back National League Ontario titles in 1974 and 1975. He also played college soccer at York University.

In 2000, Iarusci was part of the first class inducted by the Canada Soccer Hall of Fame. He was later honoured by the Toronto Azzurri SC Wall of Fame.

CANADA RECORDS

INT'L RECORDS	MP	MS	MIN	G	A
1976 CANADA	5	5	450		
1977 CANADA	5	4	405		1a
1980 CANADA	10	9	-	1g	
1981 CANADA	9	9	-	1g	1a
1983 CANADA	2	2	180		
8 SEASONS	**31**	**29**	**n/a**	**2g**	**2a**
FWC QUALIFIERS	*18*	*18*	*1620*	*2g*	*2a*

FIFA WORLD CUP QUALIFIERS • Robert Iarusci helped Canada draw Mexico four times in FIFA World Cup Qualifiers: a 0-0 draw in Toluca in 1976; a 1-1 draw at Exhibition Stadium in Toronto in 1980; a 1-1 draw at Estadio Azteca in 1980; and a 1-1 draw in Tegucigalpa, Honduras in the 1981 Concacaf Final Round.

MIDFIELDER

DANIEL IMHOF

Born: 1977-11-22, Wil, SUI. Grew up in Smithers, BC, CAN. Height 178 cm.

1 FIFA Confederations Cup: Group phase in 2001
3 cycles FIFA World Cup Qualifiers: 2000, 2004, 2008
1st #CANMNT: 2000-10-09 at Winnipeg, MB, CAN (v. PAN)

CANADA HIGHLIGHTS

Daniel Imhof made 36 international "A" appearances across 11 years from 2000 to 2010 with Canada. He represented Canada across three cycles of FIFA World Cup Qualifiers and two editions of the Concacaf Gold Cup, including a third-place finish at the 2002 edition.

After helping Canada finish in fourth place at the 1999 Pan American Games in Winnipeg, he made his international "A" debut on 9 October 2000 in that same city in FIFA World Cup Qualifiers against Panama. He recorded his first assist at the 2002 Concacaf Gold Cup (on Kevin McKenna's match winner against Haiti) and then got two more assists in 2003 friendly matches (a Kevin McKenna goal against Libya as well as a Tomasz Radzinski goal against the Czech Republic).

CLUB HIGHLIGHTS

Imhof made over 200 club appearances with FC St. Gallen across two stints in Switzerland. He helped the club win the Nationalliga A in 1999-2000 as well as the second tier Challenge League in 2011-12 (with promotion back up to the top division).

Imhof played his youth soccer in British Columbia, then turned pro with FC Wil in 1998-99. In Germany, he played four seasons in the Bundesliga with VfL Bochum after they won promotion and the 2.Bundesliga title in 2005-06.

CANADA RECORDS

"A" RECORDS	MP	MS	MIN	G	A
2000 CANADA	2	2	179		
2001 CANADA	4	3	298		
2002 CANADA	6	6	474		1a
2003 CANADA	9	9	780		2a
2004 CANADA	8	8	675		
2005 CANADA	3	3	221		
2007 CANADA	2	1	135		
2008 CANADA	1	0	17		
2010 CANADA	1	1	90		
11 SEASONS	36	33	2869		3a
FWC QUALIFIERS	9	9	764		
GOLD CUP	6	6	483		1a

CONFEDERATIONS	MP	MS	MIN
2001 FIFA CC	2	2	153

2001 FIFA CONFEDERATIONS CUP • Daniel Imhof was just 23 years old when he made two appearances at the 2001 FIFA Confederations Cup in Japan. He played a little more than an hour in the 3-0 loss to the hosts Japan and then the full 90 minutes in the 2-0 loss to Cameroon.

10

SIMEON JACKSON

FORWARD

Born: 1987-03-28, Kingston, JAM. Grew up in Mississauga, ON, CAN. Height 172 cm. Dominant right foot.

3 cycles FIFA World Cup Qualifiers: 2008, 2011-12, 2015-16
1st #CANMNT: 2009-05-30 at Larnaka, CYP (v. CYP)
1st Goal: 2009-05-30 at Larnaka, CYP (v. CYP)

CANADA HIGHLIGHTS

Simeon Jackson has made 49 international "A" appearances across 10 years from 2008 to 2017, including three cycles of FIFA World Cup Qualifiers and four editions of the Concacaf Gold Cup. He has scored six career goals and was Canada's top goalscorer across 2011-12 FIFA World Cup Qualifiers. He helped Canada reach the Quarterfinals at the 2009 Concacaf Gold Cup, the same year he was named Canada Soccer's Player of the Year.

After Jackson represented Canada at the FIFA U-20 World Cup Canada 2007, he got his first call up to the Men's National Team in 2008 for FIFA World Cup Qualifiers. He made his international "A" debut the following year in Larnaka where he scored the 1-0 match winner against Cyprus. He scored a hat trick in 2011 against St. Lucia in FIFA World Cup Qualifiers.

CLUB HIGHLIGHTS

Jackson helped Norwich City FC win promotion from England's Championship in 2010-11 to the Premier League. He then played two seasons in England's top division. He played in Germany's Bundesliga with Eintracht Braunschweig.

Jackson has already scored more than 100 goals from all levels in the United Kingdom across his professional career. Alongside his three seasons at Norwich City FC in the Championship and Premier League, he also played for Millwall FC and Blackburn Rovers FC in the Championship.

CANADA RECORDS

"A" RECORDS	MP	MS	MIN	G	A
2008 CANADA	0	0	0		
2009 CANADA	8	3	361	1g	
2010 CANADA	5	4	357	1g	
2011 CANADA	12	9	808	4g	2a
2012 CANADA	8	5	454		
2013 CANADA	6	3	228		
2014 CANADA	3	2	195		
2015 CANADA	3	0	48		
2016 CANADA	3	1	94		
2017 CANADA	1	1	75		
10 SEASONS	**49**	**28**	**2620**	**6g**	**2a**
FWC QUALIFIERS	*12*	*8*	*708*	*4g*	*2a*
GOLD CUP	*8*	*2*	*375*		

PLAYER OF THE YEAR • Simeon Jackson won Canada Soccer Player of the Year honours in 2009 when he scored 23 goals for club and country. On 23 May, he scored the 1-0 match winner that earned Gillingham FC promotion to League One. Exactly one week later, he scored Canada's 1-0 match winner in his international debut against Cyprus.

CENTRE BACK

DEJAN JAKOVIĆ

4

Born: 1985-07-16, Karlovac, CRO. Grew up in Etobicoke, ON, CAN. Height 187 cm. Dominant right foot.

3 cycles FIFA World Cup Qualifiers: 2008, 2012, 2015-16
1st #CANMNT: 2008-01-30 at Fort-de-France, MTQ (v. MTQ)
1st Goal: 2017-07-07 at Harrison, NJ, USA (v. GUF)

CANADA HIGHLIGHTS

Dejan Jaković was one of Canada's captains at the 2017 Concacaf Gold Cup when they reached the Quarterfinals for the first time in eight years. In all, he made 41 career international "A" appearances across 13 years with Canada and started four matches wearing the captain's armband. He featured in three cycles of FIFA World Cup Qualifiers and three editions of the Concacaf Gold Cup.

Six weeks after he made his National Team debut in January 2008, he helped Canada climb to within a win of qualifying for the Beijing 2008 Olympic Games.

Jaković wore the captain's armband for his last international match on 24 March 2018.

CLUB HIGHLIGHTS

With Los Angeles FC, Jaković was a 2019 MLS Supporters' Shield winner and 2020 Concacaf Champions League finalist. It was his second stint in MLS after five seasons with D.C. United where he won the 2013 US Open Cup.

After playing his youth soccer in Ontario, he played college soccer at the University of Alabama-Birmingham and then turned pro in Serbia with Red Star Belgrade in 2008.

After five years with D.C. United, Jaković moved to Japan where he played three seasons with S-Pulse Shimizu. After his return to North America, he played for the New York Cosmos, Los Angeles FC, Las Vegas Lights, and Forge FC Hamilton.

CANADA RECORDS

"A" RECORDS	MP	MS	MIN	G	A
2008 CANADA	1	0	22		
2009 CANADA	5	5	405		
2010 CANADA	3	3	270		
2011 CANADA	2	2	129		
2012 CANADA	1	1	90		
2013 CANADA	5	5	450		
2014 CANADA	1	0	45		
2015 CANADA	9	9	810		
2016 CANADA	6	5	495		
2017 CANADA	7	7	585	1g	
2018 CANADA	1	1	59		1a
2020 CANADA	0	0	0		
13 SEASONS	**41**	**38**	**3360**	**1g**	**1a**
FWC QUALIFIERS	*5*	*5*	*450*		
GOLD CUP	*9*	*9*	*820*	*1g*	

● ● ●

1st INTERNATIONAL GOAL • Dejan Jaković scored his first international goal in Canada's opening match at the 2017 Concacaf Gold Cup. He scored the opening goal of a 4-2 victory over French Guiana after a free kick from Scott Arfield. In that same match, 16-year old Alphonso Davies scored his first two international goals in the second half.

3

ANTE JAZIĆ

LEFT BACK

Born: 1976-02-27, Halifax, NS, CAN. Grew up in Bedford, NS, CAN. Height 180 cm. Dominant left foot.

3 cycles FIFA World Cup Qualifiers: 2004, 2008, 2011-12
1st #CANMNT: 1998-05-18 at Toronto, ON, CAN (v. MKD)
1st Goal: 2008-06-04 at Sunrise, FL, USA (v. PAN)

CANADA HIGHLIGHTS

Ante Jazić played every Canada minute at the 2007 Concacaf Gold when Canada reached the Semifinals. In all, he made 35 career international "A" appearances across 15 years from 1998 to 2012, including two starts for Canada wearing the captain's armband. He became Canada's oldest outfield player ever in FIFA World Cup Qualifiers in 2012.

Jazić was just 22 years old when he made his international "A" debut on 18 May 1998 against Macedonia at Toronto's Varsity Stadium. He scored his first Canada goal on 4 June 2008 in a 2-2 draw with Panama.

CLUB HIGHLIGHTS

Jazic played 17 seasons as a pro footballer in Croatia, Austria, Russia and the United States. He won the Croatian Cup in 2000 and played in UEFA Cup competition with both HNK Hajduk Split and SK Rapid Wien.

He played the last eight seasons of his career in Major League Soccer where he became the first Canadian fullback to play 10,000 MLS minutes. He split those seasons between LA Galaxy and Chivas USA and recorded a career-best seven assists during the 2011 season.

Before turning pro, he won the 1996 CIAU Championship with Dalhousie University. He was a runner up at Canada Soccer's 1995 National Championships with Halifax King of Donair. He won a Bronze Medal with Nova Scotia at the 1993 Canada Games.

CANADA RECORDS

"A" RECORDS	MP	MS	MIN	G	A
1998 CANADA	1	0	36		
1999 CANADA	1	0	22		
2003 CANADA	3	3	225		
2004 CANADA	7	7	616		
2005 CANADA	1	1	59		
2006 CANADA	3	2	141		
2007 CANADA	6	6	540		
2008 CANADA	1	0	45	1g	
2010 CANADA	1	1	90		
2011 CANADA	4	4	360		
2012 CANADA	7	7	583		2a
15 SEASONS	**35**	**31**	**2717**	**1g**	**2a**
FWC QUALIFIERS	15	15	1336		2a
GOLD CUP	5	5	450		

FIFA WORLD CUP QUALIFIERS • Ante Jazić represented Canada in three cycles of FIFA World Cup Qualifiers. During 2011-12 FIFA World Cup Qualifiers, he earned Player of the Match honours in a 0-0 home draw with Puerto Rico and then got two assists in a 3-0 home win over Cuba.

FORWARD

GLEN JOHNSON

8

Born: 1951-04-22, Vancouver, BC, CAN. Height 175 cm. Dominant right foot.

2 cycles FIFA World Cup Qualifiers: 1972, 1976
1st #CANMNT: 1972-08-20 at St. John's, NL, CAN (v. USA)
1st Goal: 1972-08-20 at St. John's, NL, CAN (v. USA)

CANADA SOCCER HALL OF FAME

Glen Johnson represented Canada in two cycles of FIFA World Cup Qualifiers across five years from 1972 to 1976. He played in every minute of Canada's 1972 campaign against USA and Mexico.

In 1976, Johnson faced both USA and Mexico once again in FIFA World Cup Qualifiers, including an important 0-0 away draw against Mexico that moved Canada into a playoff against the US to get through to the Concacaf Final Round. He was still just 25 years old when he made his last Canada appearance at Estadio La Bombonera in Toluca, Mexico.

In 1974, Johnson was the first player signed by the expansion Vancouver Whitecaps and he was just 23 years old when he made his NASL debut in the club's first match on 5 May.

On either side of a four-year NASL career, he played his soccer in British Columbia in the Mainland League, Pacific Coast League, Western Canada League, BC Premier League and BC League. He was the Western Canada League's second-highest goalscorer in 1969, despite leaving for England before the end of the season.

Johnson played for West Bromwich Albion in the Football League First Division and Central League Reserves Division. He was 19 years old when he made his First Division debut on 22 August 1970.

CANADA RECORDS

INT'L RECORDS	MP	MS	MIN	G	A
1972 CANADA	4	4	360	1g	1a
1973 CANADA	2	2	170		
1976 CANADA	2	2	180		
5 SEASONS	**8**	**8**	**710**	**1g**	**1a**
FWC QUALIFIERS	6	6	540	1g	1a

1st INTERNATIONAL GOAL • Glen Johnson scored in his international debut at King George V Park in St. John's, a famous 3-2 win over the United States in 1972 FIFA World Cup Qualifiers. Johnson scored Canada's third goal on a scissors kick to the delight of the sold-out Sunday afternoon crowd.

58 | Canadian Soccer

WILL JOHNSON

MIDFIELDER

Born: 1987-01-21, Toronto, ON, CAN. Grew up in Chicago, IL, USA. Height 178 cm. Dominant right foot.

3 cycles FIFA World Cup Qualifiers: 2008, 2011-12, 2015-16
1st #CANMNT: 2005-11-16 at Hesperange, LUX (v. LUX)
1st Goal: 2011-09-02 at Toronto, ON, CAN (v. LCA)

CANADA HIGHLIGHTS

Will Johnson made 45 career international "A" appearances for Canada across 15 years from 2005 to 2019, including three cycles of FIFA World Cup Qualifiers and four editions of the Concacaf Gold Cup. He helped Canada reach the Concacaf Gold Cup Quarterfinals in both 2009 and 2019. He won Canada Soccer's Player of the Year award in 2013.

Johnson played every Canada minute of back-to-back FIFA U-20 Worlds Cups at Netherlands 2005 and Canada 2007. With the U-23 squad at the 2008 Concacaf Olympic Qualifiers, he was named a tournament all-star after he led Canada with three goals and got them to within a win from qualifying for Beijing 2008.

CLUB HIGHLIGHTS

Johnson was a two-time MLS Cup winner in Major League Soccer, lifting the Anschutz Trophy in 2009 with Real Salt Lake and 2015 with Portland Timbers FC. He also finished as a Concacaf Champions League finalist with Real Salt Lake in 2010-11. He scored the MLS Goal of the Year in 2008 and was an MLS Best XI all-star in 2013.

With Toronto FC, he won the 2016 Canadian Championship and 2016 MLS Eastern Conference playoff trophy. In Europe, he played for sc Heerenveen and De Graafschap in the Netherlands.

CANADA RECORDS

"A" RECORDS	MP	MS	MIN	G	A
2005 CANADA	1	0	6		
2006 CANADA	2	0	27		
2007 CANADA	1	0	6		
2008 CANADA	1	1	90		
2009 CANADA	5	5	372		1
2010 CANADA	3	3	243		1
2011 CANADA	11	10	760	1	3
2012 CANADA	7	7	601	2	
2013 CANADA	3	3	231		1
2015 CANADA	4	4	341	1	1
2016 CANADA	3	3	270		
2017 CANADA	2	2	113		
2019 CANADA	2	2	150		
15 SEASONS	**45**	**40**	**3210**	**4**	**7**
FWC QUALIFIERS	*17*	*16*	*1315*	*3*	*3*
GOLD CUP	*9*	*9*	*656*		
NATIONS LEAGUE	*1*	*1*	*90*		

PLAYER OF THE YEAR • Will Johnson won Canada Soccer Player of the Year honours in 2013, the same year he was named to the MLS Best XI. He led all Canadians that year in MLS minutes, goals and tackles. At the Concacaf Gold Cup, he wore the captain's armband for the first time.

RIGHT BACK

ALISTAIR JOHNSTON

Born: 1998-10-08, North Vancouver, BC, CAN. Grew up in Aurora, ON, CAN. Height 180 cm. Dominant right foot.

1 FIFA World Cup: Group phase at Qatar 2022
1 Concacaf medal: Silver in 2022-23 CNL
1st place FIFA World Cup Qualifiers in 2021-22
1st #CANMNT: 2021-03-25 at Orlando, FL, USA (v. BER)
1st Goal: 2021-03-29 at Bradenton, FL, USA (v. CAY)

CANADA HIGHLIGHTS

Alistair Johnston is a Canada record holder after he set the Men's National Team mark with 31 consecutive international "A" appearances from 2021 to 2022. Across two years, he helped Canada win the Concacaf Final Round of FIFA World Cup Qualifiers, featured in all three Canada matches at the 2022 FIFA World Cup in Qatar, and won a Concacaf Silver Medal at the 2022-23 Concacaf Nations League Finals. Through December 2023, he has made 39 international "A" appearances, scored one goal and recorded two assists.

Johnston was 22 years old when he made his international "A" debut in a 5-1 win over Bermuda on 25 March 2021 in FIFA World Cup Qualifiers. He scored his first goal four days later in a win over the Cayman Islands. In Canada's opening match of the 2021-22 Concacaf Final Round, he earned Canada's Player of the Match honours in a 1-1 home draw against Honduras.

Across 13 months of FIFA World Cup Qualifiers, he led Canada with 19 matches, 15 starts (tied), and 1,376 minutes.

CELTIC FC

Johnston joined Celtic FC after the 2022 FIFA World Cup and quickly won the Premiership, Scottish Cup and Scottish League Cup in his first European season.

Before moving to Europe, he was CF Montréal's Defensive Player of the Season in 2022 after the club finished third overall in the MLS. He previously played his first two MLS seasons with Nashville SC and led all Canadians in MLS minutes as a rookie in 2020.

CANADA RECORDS

"A" RECORDS	MP	MS	MIN	G	A
2021 CANADA	18	16	1417	1g	2a
2022 CANADA	15	13	1173		
2023 CANADA	6	5	386		
UNTIL DEC.2023	39	34	2976	1g	2a
FWC QUALIFIERS	19	15	1376	1g	2a
GOLD CUP	5	5	423		
NATIONS LEAGUE	7	6	485		

FIFA WORLD CUP	MP	MS	MIN
2022 FIFA WC	3	3	270

2022 FIFA WORLD CUP • Alistair Johnston played in every Canada minute at the FIFA World Cup in Qatar, the nation's first participation on the world's biggest stage in 36 years. Across three group matches, he ranked second on Canada with 20 possession regains in defensive actions, 43 line breaks from possession, and six crosses from open play.

14

MARK-ANTHONY KAYE

MIDFIELDER

Born: 1994-12-02, Toronto, ON, CAN.   Height 185 cm. Dominant left foot.

1 FIFA World Cup: Group phase at Qatar 2022
1st place FIFA World Cup Qualifiers in 2021-22
1st #CANMNT: 2017-06-13 at Montréal, QC, CAN (v. CUW)
1st Goal: 2021-03-29 at Bradenton, FL, USA (v. CAY)

CANADA HIGHLIGHTS

Mark-Anthony Kaye represented Canada at the 2022 FIFA World Cup in Qatar after he helped Canada finish in first place in the 2021-22 Concacaf Final Round of FIFA World Cup Qualifiers. Through December 2023, he has already made 42 international "A" appearances, scored two goals and recorded seven assists. He has also reached the knockout phase of the Concacaf Gold Cup three times.

After playing for Canada's U-23 side, Kaye made his international "A" debut on 13 June 2017 in a 2-1 home win over Curaçao at Montréal's Stade Saputo. The following month, he got his first start in a 1-1 draw with Costa Rica at the Concacaf Gold Cup. In the 2021 Concacaf Gold Cup Semifinals, he got the assist on Canada's lone goal in a 2-1 loss to Mexico.

NEW ENGLAND REVOLUTION

Kaye joined the New England Revolution midway through his sixth MLS season in July 2023. With Los Angeles FC, he was an MLS Supporters' Shield winner in 2019 and a Concacaf Champions League finalist in 2020. He also played in the 2019 MLS All-Star Game.

Before joining New England, Kaye also played in the MLS for the Colorado Rapids and Toronto FC. He previously played for Louisville City FC where he won the 2017 USL Cup.

CANADA RECORDS

"A" RECORDS	MP	MS	MIN	G	A
2017 CANADA	5	2	230		
2018 CANADA	1	1	45		
2019 CANADA	8	7	532		3a
2020 CANADA	0	0	0		
2021 CANADA	16	12	1011	2g	4a
2022 CANADA	9	5	358		
2023 CANADA	3	0	67		
UNTIL DEC.UG.2023	42	27	2243	2g	7a
FWC QUALIFIERS	15	11	855	2g	3a
GOLD CUP	10	7	602		2a
NATIONS LEAGUE	8	4	349		1a

FIFA WORLD CUP	MP	MS	MIN		
2022 FIFA WC	1	1	60		

2022 FIFA WORLD CUP • Mark-Anthony Kaye represented Canada at the 2022 FIFA World Cup in Qatar where he got the start in their third group match against Morocco. He completed 50 of 59 passes in 60 minutes of action as one of Canada's midfielders in the 2-1 loss at Al Thumama Stadium.

LEFT BACK

MIKE KLUKOWSKI

Born: 1981-05-27, Amsterdam, AUT. Grew up in Oshawa, ON, CAN. Height 185 cm. Dominant left foot.

3 cycles FIFA World Cup Qualifiers: 2004, 2008, 2012
1st #CANMNT: 2003-02-12 at Tripoli, LBY (v. LBY)

CANADA HIGHLIGHTS

Mike Klukowski made 36 career international appearances across 10 years, including three cycles of FIFA World Cup Qualifiers and two editions of the Concacaf Gold Cup. He was a Concacaf tournament all-star in 2009 when Canada reached the Quarterfinals.

At the youth level, he represented Canada at the FIFA World Youth Championship Argentina 2001.

Klukowski was just 21 years old when he made his international "A" debut in 2003 in a 4-2 away win over Libya. He got his first start over a year later in a 4-0 home win over Belize in 2004 FIFA World Cup Qualifiers.

CLUB HIGHLIGHTS

Klukowski won the Championnat de Belgique, the Coupe Belgique (twice) and the Supercoupe de Belgique. He spent three seasons at RAA Louviéroise where he won the Cup in 2003, then six-plus seasons at Club Brugge KV where he won the League in 2004-05, the Supercup in 2005 and the Cup in 2007. He also featured in the UEFA Cup, Europa League, and UEFA Champions League Qualifying.

Klukowski grew up playing soccer in Ontario before he moved to France for the 1998-99 season. After his time in Belgium, he played two seasons in Turkey. He then won the Cypriot First Division title in 2012-13 with APOEL Nicosia.

CANADA RECORDS

"A" RECORDS	MP	MS	MIN	G	A
2003 CANADA	1	0	30		
2004 CANADA	2	1	100		
2005 CANADA	3	2	225		
2006 CANADA	2	2	87		
2007 CANADA	2	2	180		
2008 CANADA	10	10	855		1a
2009 CANADA	6	6	540		1a
2010 CANADA	2	2	154		
2011 CANADA	5	5	450		
2012 CANADA	3	2	182		
10 SEASONS	**36**	**32**	**2803**		**2a**
FWC QUALIFIERS	11	11	945		
GOLD CUP	5	5	450		1a

FIFA WORLD CUP QUALIFIERS • Mike Klukowski played in a career-high 10 international matches in 2008 including seven of Canada's eight FIFA World Cup Qualifiers. He ranked second on Canada in minutes played behind only Paul Stalteri. In a May 2008 friendly against Brazil (a 3-2 loss), he recorded the assist on Canada's first goal by Rob Friend.

7

VICTOR KODELJA

FORWARD / FB

Born: 1951-11-26, Capua Casserta, ITA. Grew up in Vancouver, BC, CAN. Height 180 cm. Dominant left foot.

1 cycle FIFA World Cup Qualifiers: 1972, 1976-77
1st #CANMNT: 1974-04-12 at Hamilton, BER (v. BER)
1st Goal: 1974-10-28 at Budapest, HUN (v. HUN U-23)

 CANADA SOCCER HALL OF FAME

Victor Kodelja represented Canada 14 times across four years from his international debut on 12 April 1974 through to the Concacaf Final Round of FIFA World Cup Qualifiers in 1977. He scored for Canada on 28 October 1974 in a 1-1 away draw with Hungary's U-23 side at Budapest.

Across those 14 Canada matches, he made eight international "A" appearances including the Concacaf Final Round of FIFA World Cup Qualifiers in 1977. He made his last appearance in a 2-1 win over Suriname at Estadio Azteca in Mexico.

At the professional level, Kodelja won the 1984 NASL Championship with the Chicago Sting in the league's final season.

In all, he played eight seasons across 11 NASL years from 1974 to 1984 with the Vancouver Whitecaps, San Antonio Thunder / Team Hawaii, San Jose Earthquakes, Calgary Boomers, Toronto Blizzard and Chicago Sting. He helped Toronto reach Soccer Bowl '83 one year before he won it all with Chicago at Soccer Bowl '84.

Alongside his NASL career, he also played indoor soccer with Calgary and Toronto.

Before turning pro, Kodelja played in British Columbia in the Pacific Coast League, BC Premier League and BC League. With Vancouver Columbus FC, he won league and playoff titles as well as the 1969 Canada Soccer Football Championship for the Challenge Trophy. He was the hero of the 1969 Western Final when he scored Vancouver's 4-3 winner in extra time.

CANADA RECORDS

INT'L RECORDS	MP	MS	MIN	G	A
1974 CANADA	7	7	-	1g	
1975 CANADA	3	2	207		
1976 CANADA	1	1	60		
1977 CANADA	3	3	225		
4 SEASONS	**14**	**13**	**n/a**	**1g**	
FWC QUALIFIERS	*3*	*3*	*195*		

FIFA WORLD CUP QUALIFIERS • Victor Kodelja made his FIFA World Cup Qualifiers debut in Port-au-Prince when Canada won 3-0 over USA just three days before Christmas 1976 in Haiti to reach the Conacaf Final Round. Canada finished fourth in the region in 1977, but only first-place Mexico qualified for the 1978 FIFA World Cup.

FORWARD

CYLE LARIN

17

Born: 1995-04-17 at Brampton, ON, CAN. Height 188 cm. Dominant right foot.

1 FIFA World Cup: Group phase at Qatar 2022
1 Concacaf medal: Silver in 2022-23 CNL
1st place FIFA World Cup Qualifiers in 2021-22
1st #CANMNT: 2014-05-23 at Ritzing, AUT (v. BUL)
1st Goal: 2015-03-30 at Bayamón, PUR (v. PUR)

CANADA HIGHLIGHTS

Cyle Larin is Canada's record holder with already 28 international "A" goals through December 2023, including 17 goals in FIFA World Cup Qualifiers and a single-year record 14 goals in 2021. Across two years, he helped Canada win the Concacaf Final Round of FIFA World Cup Qualifiers and win a Concacaf Silver Medal at the 2022-23 Nations League Finals. He was Canada's runner up in Player of the Year voting in both 2015 and 2016.

Larin was 19 years old when he made his international "A" debut in a 1-1 draw with Bulgaria at Ritzing in Austria. Less than a year later, he scored his first goal in a 3-0 away win over Puerto Rico. In the most recent cycle of FIFA World Cup Qualifiers ahead of Qatar 2022, his 13 goals ranked second in the world behind only UAE's Ali Mabkhout (14 goals).

RCD MALLORCA

Larin has already scored more than 100 pro goals before joining RCD Mallorca ahead of the 2023-24 La Liga season. In Turkey, he won the Süper Lig, the Turkish Cup and the Turkish Supercup with Beşiktaş JK. In Belgium, he won the Supercoupe de Belgique with Club Brugge KV.

Before moving to Europe, Larin was the second-highest scoring Canadian in MLS history after just three seasons. He was the MLS Rookie of the Year in 2015.

CANADA RECORDS

"A" RECORDS	MP	MS	MIN	G	A
2014 CANADA	3	0	55		
2015 CANADA	11	8	630	4g	
2016 CANADA	5	5	401	1g	
2017 CANADA	4	3	214		
2018 CANADA	4	1	171	3g	
2019 CANADA	4	2	155		
2020 CANADA	0	0	0		
2021 CANADA	13	11	842	14g	
2022 CANADA	14	10	752	3g	1a
2023 CANADA	7	7	504	3g	1a
UNTIL DEC.2023	65	47	3724	28g	2a
FWC QUALIFIERS	26	22	1757	17g	
GOLD CUP	8	7	454	3g	
NATIONS LEAGUE	10	8	599	3g	2a

FIFA WORLD CUP	MP	MS	MIN
2022 FIFA WC	3	2	137

CANADA GOALS RECORD • Cyle Larin set Canada Soccer's Men's National Team's international goals record on 28 March 2023 when he scored two goals at BMO Field in Toronto. He broke John Catliff's record (26) with his first goal, a right-footed shot in the 4-1 victory as Canada qualified for the 2022-23 Concacaf Nations League Semifinals.

64 | Canadian Soccer

22

RICHIE LARYEA

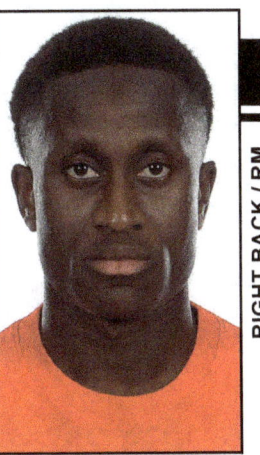

RIGHT BACK / RM

Born: 1995-01-07, Toronto, ON, CAN.   Height 175 cm.
Dominant right foot.

1 FIFA World Cup: Group phase at Qatar 2022
1 Concacaf medal: Silver in 2022-23 CNL
1st place FIFA World Cup Qualifiers in 2021-22
1st #CANMNT: 2019-09-07 at Toronto, ON, CAN (v. CUB)
1st Goal: 2021-03-25 at Orlando, FL, USA (v. BER)

CANADA HIGHLIGHTS

Richie Laryea has helped Canada win the Concacaf Final Round of FIFA World Cup Qualifiers, participate in their first men's FIFA World Cup in 36 years, and win a Concacaf Silver Medal in the region's Nations League Finals. Through December 2023, he has already made 48 international "A" appearances, scored one goal and recorded six assists. He has also played in two editions of the Concacaf Gold Cup.

Laryea was 24 years old when he made his international "A" debut in 2019-20 Concacaf Nations League, a home 6-0 win over Cuba at Toronto's BMO Field. The following month, he helped Canada beat the United States for the first time in 34 years, a 2-0 home win at Toronto.

In 2021, he scored his first international "A" goal in his first FIFA World Cup Qualifiers match, a 5-1 win over Bermuda. During FIFA World Cup Qualifiers, he earned Player of the Match honours at home against El Salvador and away against Costa Rica.

TORONTO FC

Laryea rejoined Toronto FC ahead of the 2024 MLS season from Nottingham Forest FC in England. He played the back half of the 2023 season with Vancouver Whitecaps FC.

Laryea played his youth soccer in Ontario. He was 22 years old when he made his MLS debut on 24 June 2017 with Orlando City SC.

CANADA RECORDS

"A" RECORDS	MP	MS	MIN	G	A
2019 CANADA	4	4	360		
2020 CANADA	2	2	107		
2021 CANADA	16	14	1248	1g	2a
2022 CANADA	15	9	832		1a
2023 CANADA	11	10	957		3a
UNTIL DEC.2023	48	39	3504	1g	6a
FWC QUALIFIERS	17	14	1233	1g	2a
GOLD CUP	9	8	776		
NATIONS LEAGUE	12	10	929		4a

FIFA WORLD CUP	MP	MS	MIN		
2022 FIFA WC	3	2	161		

2022 FIFA WORLD CUP • Richie Laryea featured in all three Canada matches at the FIFA World Cup in Qatar, Canada's first participation at the world's biggest men's tournament since 1986. He had starts against Belgium and Croatia, then featured in the second half against Morocco.

MIDFIELDER / FB

NIK LEDGERWOOD

Born: 1985-01-16, Lethbridge, AB, CAN. Height 175 cm. Dominant right foot.

3 cycles FIFA World Cup Qualifiers: 2008, 2011-12, 2015-16
1st #CANMNT: 2007-08-22 at Reykjavík, ISL (v. ISL)
1st Goal: 2016-09-06 at Vancouver, BC, CAN (v. SLV)

CANADA HIGHLIGHTS

Nik Ledgerwood wore the captain's armband when he made his milestone 50th Canada appearance on 22 March 2017, which was also his last Canada match after 11 international seasons.

Across his career, he played in three cycles of FIFA World Cup Qualifiers and three editions of the Concacaf Gold Cup. He led Canada in minutes played in 2013.

Ledgerwood captained Canada's U-20 side at the 2005 FIFA World Youth Championship and he helped the U-23 squad get to within a victory of reaching Beijing 2008 Olympic Games. He also featured in one match at the 2003 FIFA World Youth Championship when Canada reached the Quarterfinals.

CLUB HIGHLIGHTS

Ledgerwood played his club football in Germany, Sweden and Canada, notably in Germany's 2.Bundesliga with TSV 1860 München, SV Wacker Burghausen and FSV Frankfurt.

He was an original member of Calgary's Cavalry FC where he helped them finish as the Canadian Premier League's runners up in 2019 and 2021. He also helped Cavalry FC reach the Canadian Championship Semifinals in 2019.

Before joining Calgary, he initially returned home from Europe to join FC Edmonton in the NASL.

CANADA RECORDS

"A" RECORDS	MP	MS	MIN	G	A
2007 CANADA	1	0	18		
2008 CANADA	1	1	90		
2009 CANADA	1	1	90		
2010 CANADA	3	2	162		
2011 CANADA	8	8	700		
2012 CANADA	8	6	482		
2013 CANADA	11	11	872		
2014 CANADA	4	3	248		
2015 CANADA	8	8	667		1a
2016 CANADA	4	3	230	1g	
2017 CANADA	1	1	90		
11 SEASONS	50	44	3649	1g	1a
FWC QUALIFIERS	16	13	1107	1g	1a
GOLD CUP	8	8	720		

● ● ●

1st INTERNATIONAL GOAL • Nik Ledgerwood scored his first international "A" goal during 2015-16 FIFA World Cup Qualifiers with Canada. He got an assist in Canada's 3-0 home win over Belize in September 2015, then scored the match winner in a 3-1 victory over El Salvador one year later in September 2016.

5

BOB LENARDUZZI

RIGHT BACK / M

Born: 1955-05-01, Vancouver, BC, CAN. Height 185 cm. Dominant right foot.

1 FIFA World Cup: Group phase at Mexico 1986
1 Olympic Games: Quarterfinals at Los Angeles 1984
1 Concacaf title: 1985 Concacaf Championship
3 cycles FIFA World Cup Qualifiers: 1976-77, 1980-81, 1985
1st #CANMNT: 1973-08-01 at Toronto, ON, CAN (v. POL)
1st Goal: 1976-12-22 at Port-au-Prince, HAI (v. USA)

CANADA SOCCER HALL OF FAME

Bob Lenarduzzi made 60 international appearances for Canada, ranked second all-time after his last Canada match on 9 June 1986 at the FIFA World Cup in Mexico. He helped Canada lift the Greg Kafaty Trophy at the 1985 Concacaf Championship when Canada qualified for the FIFA World Cup for the first time ever at King George V Park in St. John's. He was also in the Canada squad 17 months earlier when Canada qualified for the Olympic Games at Victoria's Royal Athletic Park.

Lenarduzzi was just 18 years old when he made his international debut on 1 August 1973 in front of a record Canada crowd at Toronto's Varsity Stadium against Poland. He scored his first Canada goal in a 3-0 playoff win over the United States at Port-au-Prince, Haiti in FIFA World Cup Qualifiers just three days before Christmas 1976. The following year, he scored the match winner against Guatemala in the 1977 Concacaf Final Round at Estadio Azteca in Mexico.

Lenarduzzi won the 1979 NASL Championship with the Vancouver Whitecaps. He was a two-time NASL Second Team All-Star and won the 1978 NASL North American Player of the Year Award. With the 86ers, he won the 1988 CSL Championship in his final year as a player. Before turning pro, he played youth soccer in British Columbia and then England.

CANADA RECORDS

INT'L RECORDS		MP	MS	MIN	G	A
1972	CANADA	0	0	0		
1973	CANADA	2	2	180		
1976	CANADA	5	5	450	1g	1a
1977	CANADA	4	4	360	1g	
1980	CANADA	10	10	-	2g	
1981	CANADA	7	7	585	1g	
1983	CANADA	4	4	360		
1984	CANADA	10	10	930		
1985	CANADA	12	12	1065		2a
1986	CANADA	6	6	495		
15 SEASONS		**60**	**60**	**n/a**	**5g**	**3a**
FWC QUALIFIERS		*25*	*25*	*2205*	*2g*	*3a*

FIFA / OLYMPIC		MP	MS	MIN
1984	OLYMPIC	4	4	390
1986	FIFA WC	3	3	270

1986 FIFA WORLD CUP • Bob Lenarduzzi played every Canada minute at the FIFA World Cup in Mexico, Canada's first participation on the world's biggest stage. Canada were impressive in their debut against the European champions France, but they ultimately lost the opener 1-0. They lost their next two matches to Hungary and the Soviet Union.

CENTRE BACK / FB

SAM LENARDUZZI

Born 1948-12-19, Udine, ITA. Grew up in Vancouver, BC, CAN. Height 178 cm. Dominant right foot.

3 cycles FIFA World Cup Qualifiers: 1968, 1972, 1976-77
1st #CANMNT: 1967-07-25 at Winnipeg, MB, CAN (v. CUB)

CANADA SOCCER HALL OF FAME

Sam Lenarduzzi was Canada's record holder with 48 career international appearances across 15 years from 1967 to 1981. He represented Canada in three cycles of FIFA World Cup Qualifiers, two cycles of Olympic Qualifiers and two editions of the Pan American Games. Across 10 years of FIFA World Cup Qualifiers from 1968 to 1977, he played in 17 of Canada's 18 matches including every Canada minute of the Concacaf Final Round in 1977.

Across his career, Lenarduzzi helped Canada beat Mexico in 1971 Olympic Qualifiers and 1976 FIFA World Cup Qualifiers, both times at Vancouver's Empire Stadium. In 1973, he was on the pitch for his brother Bobby's international debut, the first of 11 international matches in which the two brothers played together for Canada.

At the club level, Lenarduzzi was a two-time Canada Soccer Football Championship winner, at first in 1966 with the British Columbia Selects and then again in 1969 with Vancouver Columbus FC. He was also a national runner up in 1968 with Columbus FC.

Lenarduzzi played nine seasons in the North American Soccer League: five seasons alongside his brother with the Vancouver Whitecaps and then four seasons with the Toronto Blizzard.

CANADA RECORDS

INT'L RECORDS	MP	MS	MIN	G	A
1967 CANADA	1	0	-		
1968 CANADA	4	4	360		
1971 CANADA	11	11	-		
1972 CANADA	4	4	-		
1973 CANADA	8	8	720		
1974 CANADA	7	7	630		
1975 CANADA	2	2	180		
1976 CANADA	4	3	336		
1977 CANADA	6	6	495		
1980 CANADA	1	1	45		
1981 CANADA	0	0	0		
15 SEASONS	**48**	**46**	**n/a**		
FWC QUALIFIERS	17	16	-		
PAN AMERICAN	8	7	-		

FIFA WORLD CUP QUALIFIERS • Sam Lenarduzzi was the first Canadian player to feature in three cycles of FIFA World Cup Qualifiers starting in 1968. He was Canada's youngest player that year and he played in every minute of their four matches. In 1967, he was just 18 years old when he made his international debut at the Pan American Games.

1

TINO LETTIERI

GOALKEEPER

Born: 1957-09-27, Torito Bari, ITA. Grew up in Montréal, QC, CAN. Height 175 cm. Dominant right foot.

1 FIFA World Cup: Group phase at Mexico 1986
2 Olympic Games: Montréal 1976, Los Angeles 1984
1 Concacaf title: 1985 Concacaf Championship
2 cycles FIFA World Cup Qualifiers: 1980-81, 1985
1st #CANMNT: 1975-07-06 at Montréal, QC, CAN (v. POL)
1st Clean Sheet: 1980-09-17 at Edmonton, AB, CAN (v. NZL)

 CANADA SOCCER HALL OF FAME

Tino Lettieri made 35 career appearances for Canada, ranked first amongst goalkeepers after his last Canada match on 9 June 1986 at the FIFA World Cup in Mexico. He represented Canada at two Olympic Games as well as the 1986 FIFA World Cup in Mexico. He was also part of the Canada squad that won the 1985 Concacaf Championship.

Lettieri was just 17 years old when he made his international debut in his hometown Montréal in the second half of a 1975 loss to Poland, the third-place team from the 1974 FIFA World Cup. While he didn't feature at the Olympic Games in 1976, he played every minute for Canada when they reached the Quarterfinals in 1984.

In 1985 FIFA World Cup Qualifiers, he posted away clean sheets against both Honduras in Tegucigalpa (a 1-0 win) and then Costa Rica in San José (a 0-0 draw).

Lettieri played more than a decade of professional soccer between the North American Soccer League, Major Indoor Soccer League, and Canadian Soccer League. In 1983 with the Vancouver Whitecaps, he was an NASL Second Team All-Star and won the NASL North American Player of the Year award.

In the MISL, he helped Strikers reach the MISL Final in 1986. He was the league's Goalkeeper of the Season in 1986-87.

CANADA RECORDS

INT'L RECORDS	MP	MS	MIN	CS
1975 CANADA	1	0	45	0 CS
1976 CANADA	1	0	45	1 CS
1980 CANADA	7	7	630	3 CS
1981 CANADA	8	8	630	3 CS
1983 CANADA	2	2	180	0 CS
1984 CANADA	9	9	840	5 CS
1985 CANADA	5	5	450	3 CS
1986 CANADA	2	2	180	0 CS
1988 CANADA	0	0	0	0 CS
14 SEASONS	**35**	**33**	**3000**	**15 CS**
FWC QUALIFIERS	*13*	*13*	*1170*	*4 CS*

FIFA / OLYMPIC	MP	MS	MIN	CS
1976 OLYMPIC	0	0	0	0 CS
1984 OLYMPIC	4	4	390	0 CS
1986 FIFA WC	2	2	180	0 CS

1984 OLYMPIC GAMES • Tino Lettieri was the only Canadian selected to both the 1976 and 1984 Olympic Football Tournaments. In 1984, he posted three-straight clean sheets in the Olympic Qualifiers. He then helped Canada reach the 1984 Quarterfinals before they were eliminated by Brazil on kicks from the penalty mark.

CENTRE BACK / M

JOHN LIMNIATIS

Born: 1967-06-24, Athens, GRE. Grew up in Athens, GRE & Montréal, QC, CAN. Height 183 cm. Dominant right foot.

3 FIFA World Cup Qualifiers: 1988, 1992-93, 1996-97
1st #CANMNT: 1987-09-30 at San Salvador, SLV (v. SLV)
1st Goal: 1991-07-03 at Los Angeles, CA, USA (v. JAM)

CANADA SOCCER HALL OF FAME

John Limniatis made 49 career international appearances, including three cycles of FIFA World Cup Qualifiers and three editions of the Concacaf Gold Cup. He helped Canada win the 1990 Three Nations Cup, reach FIFA's 1993 intercontinental playoff against Australia, and reach the Concacaf Final Round of FIFA World Cup Qualifiers in 1997.

In 1994, he featured in Canada's historic 1-1 draw with Brazil in front of a Canadian record crowd at Edmonton.

He was 20 years old when he made his international debut in San Salvador in 1997. At the 1988 Sir Stanley Matthews Cup in Toronto, he helped Canada post back-to-back clean sheets against Chile and Greece to win the tournament.

As a pro player, Limniatis won the 1994 APSL Championship and then three successive Commissioner's Cup regular season titles with the Montréal Impact. He was the A-League Defender of the Year in 1996. From 1993 to 2001, he mostly played with Montréal, but also played with the Charleston Battery and indoor Kansas City Attack.

Limniatis played his first two pro seasons in the Canadian Soccer League with the Ottawa Pioneers / Ottawa Intrepid. He then moved to Greece where he played four seasons with Aris Thessaloniki FC and one season with Panetolikos FC.

CANADA RECORDS

INT'L RECORDS	MP	MS	MIN	G	A
1987 CANADA	3	3	270		
1988 CANADA	16	15	1398		
1989 CANADA	1	1	90		
1990 CANADA	2	2	180		1a
1991 CANADA	2	2	180	1g	
1992 CANADA	7	6	433		
1993 CANADA	5	5	376		1a
1994 CANADA	5	2	196		
1995 CANADA	1	1	90		
1996 CANADA	5	1	166		
1997 CANADA	2	1	104		
11 SEASONS	**49**	**39**	**3483**	**1g**	**2a**
FWC QUALIFIERS	11	8	650		
GOLD CUP	6	4	385	1g	
3 NATIONS CUP	2	2	180		1a

1st INTERNATIONAL GOAL • John Limniatis scored his first international goal at the inaugural Concacaf Gold Cup in 1991 against Jamaica, the match winner in a 3-2 victory after Canada were already eliminated from the group phase. In all, he played six career Concacaf Gold Cup matches across three editions of the tournament from 1991 to 1996.

18

CARMINE MARCANTONIO

MIDFIELDER

Born: 1954-11-21, Castel di Sangro, ITA. Grew up in Toronto, ON, CAN. Height 175 cm. Dominant right foot.

2 cycles FIFA World Cup Qualifiers: 1976, 1980
1st #CANMNT: 1976-09-24 at Vancouver, BC, CAN (v. USA)

CANADA SOCCER HALL OF FAME

Carmine Marcantonio was selected to represent Canada in two cycles of FIFA World Cup Qualifiers. He featured in one match in 1976 and then another match 1980, both times against USA at Empire Stadium in Vancouver.

Marcantonio also featured four times for Canada in exhibition matches against club teams, including a pair of home draws against touring Peruvian side Sporting Cristal and a home 1-1 draw against the New York Cosmos in Calgary.

Before turning pro, Marcantonio played at the University of Toronto and he played several seasons with Toronto Italia FC. He was still just 20 years old when Italia FC won the National League Ontario title in 1975.

As a pro rookie in 1976, Marcantonio helped Toronto Metros-Croatia win the 1976 NASL Championship. He featured in 23 matches during the regular season as well as one match during the playoffs.

After another year with Toronto Italia FC, he then played seven seasons in the NASL from 1978 to 1984 with the Washington Diplomats, CS Manic de Montréal and New York Cosmos. He also played indoor soccer and notably won the 1980-81 MISL Championship with the New York Arrows.

Marcantonio was 14 years old when he arrived in Canada from Italy and he initially played youth soccer for Toronto Westwood Azzurri SC. In retirement, he was inducted to the Azzurri SC Wall of Fame in 2018.

CANADA RECORDS

"A" RECORDS	MP	MS	MIN
1976 CANADA	1	1	90
1980 CANADA	1	0	67
1981 CANADA	0	0	0
6 SEASONS	**2**	**1**	**157**
FWC QUALIFIERS	*2*	*1*	*157*

FIFA WORLD CUP QUALIFIERS • Carmine Marcantonio made his international "A" debut in 1976 FIFA World Cup Qualifiers in a 1-1 draw with USA at Empire Stadium in Vancouver. Four years later, he made his second FIFA World Cup Qualifiers appearance again in Vancouver against USA, albeit this time in a 2-1 win.

CENTRE BACK / W

JOHN McGRANE

17

Born: 1953-10-12, Glasgow, SCO. Grew up in Hamilton, ON, CAN. Height 178 cm. Dominant right foot.

1 Olympic Games: Group phase at Montréal 1976
2 cycles FIFA World Cup Qualifiers: 1977, 1980-81
1st #CANMNT: 1976-04-23 at Greenock, SCO (v. SCO)

CANADA SOCCER HALL OF FAME

John McGrane made 23 career international appearances from 1976 to 1981, including his Canada debut at age 22 against the Scottish Amateur Selects in Greenock. He represented Canada at their home Olympic Games at Montréal 1976 as well as back-to-back FIFA World Cup Qualifiers in 1976-77 and 1980-81. He was part of the Canadian squad that came within a goal of qualifying for the 1982 FIFA World Cup in Spain.

In Canada's first round of FIFA World Cup Qualifiers in 1980, McGrane helped Canada draw Mexico twice, first a 1-1 home draw at Toronto's Exhibition Stadium and then a 1-1 away draw at Estadio Azteca in front of some 90,000 fans in México City. He also helped Canada post a 2-1 home win over the United States at Empire Stadium in Vancouver.

McGrane was the Los Angeles Aztecs' Rookie of the Year at the start of an eight-year NASL career as a professional footballer. From 1977 to 1984, he played with the Aztecs, Manic de Montréal and Minnesota Strikers. He also played indoor soccer with the Aztecs, Manic, Chicago Sting and Strikers.

Before turning pro, he won the 1976 NAIA Championship at Simon Fraser University. He played his youth soccer in Ontario and played in the National League Ontario with Hamilton Apollo SC and Hamilton City SC.

CANADA RECORDS

INT'L RECORDS	MP	MS	MIN
1976 CANADA	6	5	-
1977 CANADA	3	2	210
1980 CANADA	8	7	-
1981 CANADA	6	4	-
4 SEASONS	**23**	**18**	**n/a**
FWC QUALIFIERS	9	8	750

OLYMPIC GAMES	MP	MS	MIN
1976 OLYMPIC	2	2	141

● ● ●

1976 OLYMPIC GAMES • John McGrane started up front for Canada at the 1976 Olympic Football Tournament in Montréal and Toronto. After the Olympic Games, he went back to Simon Fraser University and then finished the year on Canada's FIFA World Cup Qualifiers squad in Haiti just before Christmas 1976.

KEVIN McKENNA

CENTRE BACK / F

Born: 1980-01-21, Calgary, AB, CAN. Height 192 cm. Dominant right foot.

1 FIFA Confederations Cup: Group phase in 2001
4 cycles FIFA World Cup Qualifiers: 2000, 2004, 2008, 2011-12
1st #CANMNT: 2000-05-27 at Toronto, ON, CAN (v. TRI)
1st Goal: 2000-05-30 at Winnipeg, MB, CAN (v. HON)

 CANADA SOCCER HALL OF FAME

Kevin McKenna made 28 international starts for Canada wearing the captain's armband including FIFA World Cup Qualifiers and the Concacaf Gold Cup. In all, he made 63 career appearances including a third-place finish at the 2002 Concacaf Gold Cup when he was named a tournament all-star.

After representing Canada in 2000 Concacaf Olympic Qualifiers, McKenna made his international "A" debut on 27 May 2000 against Trinidad and Tobago at Toronto's Varsity Stadium. Just three days later, he scored the 2-1 match winner at Winnipeg against Honduras.

McKenna spent 16 seasons in Europe as a professional footballer. He was part of two German clubs that twice won promotion to the Bundesliga: FC Energie Cottbus in 1999-00 and 2005-06; then FC Köln in 2007-08 and 2013-14 as league winners.

He was just 19 years old when he made his 2.Bundesliga debut on 23 April 1999.

He went on to make more than 100 appearances in the Bundesliga.

In between two stints with FC Energie Cottbus, McKenna played in the Scottish Premier League where he made more than 100 appearances in Scotland's top league.

CANADA RECORDS

"A" RECORDS	MP	MS	MIN	G	A
2000 CANADA	3	3	270	1g	
2001 CANADA	4	4	360		
2002 CANADA	6	6	593	3g	
2003 CANADA	8	8	711	2g	2a
2004 CANADA	4	2	217	1g	
2005 CANADA	7	7	575	2g	
2006 CANADA	3	3	225		
2007 CANADA	2	2	180		
2008 CANADA	1	1	90		
2009 CANADA	8	8	710		
2010 CANADA	2	2	180	1g	
2011 CANADA	7	7	630		
2012 CANADA	8	8	720	1g	
13 SEASONS	**63**	**61**	**5461**	**11g**	**2a**
FWC QUALIFIERS	13	12	1100	1g	1a
GOLD CUP	16	16	1478	3g	

CONFEDERATIONS	MP	MS	MIN
2001 FIFA CC	2	2	180

2001 FIFA CONFEDERATIONS CUP • Kevin McKenna made two appearances for Canada at the 2001 FIFA Confederations Cup in Japan. After a 3-0 loss to the hosts Japan in the tournament opener, Canada drew 0-0 with Brazil in the second match. At 21 years old, he was Canada's youngest starter in both matches.

LEFT MIDFIELD

WES McLEOD

Born: 1957-10-24, Vancouver, BC, CAN. Height 175 cm. Dominant left foot.

1 Olympic Games: Group phase at Montréal 1976
2 cycles FIFA World Cup Qualifiers: 1976-77, 1980-81
1st #CANMNT: 1975-07-09 at Montréal, QC, CAN (v. POL)
1st Goal: 1981-11-21 at Tegucigalpa, HON (v. CUB)

CANADA SOCCER HALL OF FAME

Wes McLeod made 29 career international appearances from 1975 to 1985 including Canada's home Olympic Games at Montréal 1976 and two cycles of FIFA World Cup Qualifiers. He was part of the Canada squad that came within a goal of qualifying for the 1982 FIFA World Cup in Spain.

McLeod was one of two 17-year old Canada international debutants in 1975 and he was Canada's youngest player a year later at the Olympic Games in Montréal and Toronto. He was Canada's Player of the Match in the 3-1 loss to Korea DPR at Varsity Stadium.

In the 1981 Concacaf Final Round of FIFA World Cup Qualifiers, he scored his first international "A" goal in the 2-2 draw with Cuba.

McLeod was a club legend with the indoor Dallas Sidekicks where he won the 1987 MISL Championship. He spent seven seasons in Dallas and was the league's Defender of the Year in 1989-90. His Dallas jersey number 8 was retired by the club.

From 1977 to 1984, McLeod played in the North American Soccer League with the Tampa Bay Rowdies, notably reaching the playoff final in 1978 and 1979. Before turning pro, he played his youth soccer in British Columbia.

Wes McLeod's father Gordon is a former Canada international while his uncle Normie is an honoured member of the Canada Soccer Hall of Fame.

CANADA RECORDS

INT'L RECORDS	MP	MS	MIN	
1975 CANADA	1	0	-	
1976 CANADA	8	8	-	
1977 CANADA	1	1	65	
1980 CANADA	9	8	-	
1981 CANADA	7	3	454	1g
1985 CANADA	3	3	270	
11 SEASONS	**29**	**23**	**n/a**	**1g**
FWC QUALIFIERS	*9*	*9*	*797*	*1g*

OLYMPIC GAMES	MP	MS	MIN
1976 OLYMPIC	2	2	180

1976 OLYMPIC GAMES • Wes McLeod featured in every Canada minute at the 1976 Olympic Football Tournament in Montréal and Toronto. In the opener against the Soviet Union, his shot in the 88th minute led to Canada's historic first goal scored by captain Jimmy Douglas on the rebound.

COLIN MILLER

Born: 1964-10-04, Lanark, SCO. Grew up in Vancouver, BC, CAN. Height 170 cm.

1 FIFA World Cup: Group phase at Mexico 1986
3 cycles FIFA World Cup Qualifiers: 1988, 1992-93, 1996-97
1st #CANMNT: 1983-06-19 at Toronto, ON, CAN (v. SCO)
1st Goal: 1984-10-24 at Rabat, MAR (v. MAR)

CANADA SOCCER HALL OF FAME

Colin Miller wore the captain's armband more than 30 times from 1992 to 1996. He represented Canada at the 1986 FIFA World Cup, three cycles of FIFA World Cup Qualifiers, and won the 1990 Three Nations Cup. In 1994, he captained Canada for their memorable 1-1 draw with Brazil in front of a Canadian record crowd at Edmonton's Commonwealth Stadium.

Miller was just 18 years old when he made his international debut on 19 June 1983 at Toronto's Varsity Stadium against Scotland. He scored his first goal over a year later on 24 October 1984 against Morocco in Rabat.

Miller spent most of 16 professional seasons in Scotland and England from 1984 to 2000, but he also spent two seasons in the Canadian Soccer League with the Hamilton Steelers.

In Scotland, he notably featured in the UEFA Cup with Glasgow's Rangers FC. He won the Scottish First Division and promotion to Scotland's Premier League with Dunfermline Athletic. Before moving to Scotland, Miller played three seasons as a teenager in the NASL with the Toronto Blizzard.

CANADA RECORDS

INT'L RECORDS	MP	MS	MIN		
1983 CANADA	4	3	-		
1984 CANADA	3	3	270	1g	
1986 CANADA	2	2	180		
1987 CANADA	1	1	90		
1988 CANADA	1	1	90		
1989 CANADA	2	2	180		
1990 CANADA	2	1	180		
1991 CANADA	3	2	232	1g	
1992 CANADA	10	10	888	2g	
1993 CANADA	11	11	960	1g	
1994 CANADA	5	5	425		
1995 CANADA	5	5	450		1a
1996 CANADA	8	7	700		
1997 CANADA	8	8	683		
15 SEASONS	**65**	**61**	**n/a**	**5g**	**1a**
FWC QUALIFIERS	*28*	*27*	*2433*	*2g*	
GOLD CUP	*8*	*7*	*682*	*1g*	
3 NATIONS CUP	*2*	*2*	*180*		

FIFA WORLD CUP	MP	MS	MIN
1986 FIFA WC	0	0	0

1990 THREE NATIONS CUP • Colin Miller featured in every minute of action when Canada won the 1990 North American Championship in Burnaby, British Columbia. In the three-nation, round-robin series, Miller helped Canada win the opener 1-0 over USA and the second match 2-1 over Mexico.

CENTRE BACK / LB

KAMAL MILLER

4

Born: 1997-05-16, Scarborough, ON, CAN. Height 183 cm. Dominant left foot.

1 FIFA World Cup: Group phase at Qatar 2022
1 Concacaf medal: Silver in 2022-23 CNL
1st place FIFA World Cup Qualifiers in 2021-22
1st #CANMNT: 2019-06-23 at Charlotte, NC, USA (v. CUB)

CANADA HIGHLIGHTS

Kamal Miller featured in every Canada minute at the 2022 FIFA World Cup in Qatar. He helped Canada finish in first place in 2021-22 FIFA World Cup Qualifiers, then won a Concacaf Silver Medal at the Nations League Finals in 2022-23.

Miller made his international "A" debut at the 2019 Concacaf Gold Cup in a 7-0 win over Cuba. Later that year, he helped Canada beat the United States for the first time in 34 years, a 2-0 home win at Toronto's BMO Field in Concacaf Nations League. During 2021-22 FIFA World Cup Qualifiers, he helped Canada earn their first away point at Estadio Azteca in 41 years, a 1-1 draw against Mexico. At the 2022 FIFA World Cup, he earned Canada's Player of the Match honours in their opening match against Belgium.

PORTLAND TIMBERS FC

Miller is a Canadian Championship winner from two-plus seasons at CF Montréal, lifting the Voyageurs Cup in 2021 after they beat Toronto FC in the Final. In 2022, he became the first Canadian centre back to start in the MLS All-Star Game and he helped his club finish third overall in the MLS standings.

Miller was 21 years old when he made his professional debut with Orlando City SC on 2 March 2019. He joined CF Inter Miami in April 2023 and helped the club advance to the final four in the inaugural edition of the Leagues Cup between MLS and Liga MX clubs.

CANADA RECORDS

"A" RECORDS	MP	MS	MIN	G	A
2019 CANADA	3	2	182		
2020 CANADA	2	2	180		
2021 CANADA	13	12	1095		
2022 CANADA	14	12	1084		2a
2023 CANADA	9	9	840		1a
UNTIL DEC. 2023	41	37	3381		3a
FWC QUALIFIERS	13	10	952		1a
GOLD CUP	10	9	856		
NATIONS LEAGUE	8	8	693		1a

FIFA WORLD CUP	MP	MS	MIN
2022 FIFA WC	3	3	270

2022 FIFA WORLD CUP • Kamal Miller featured in every Canada minute at the FIFA World Cup in Qatar, the nation's first time in 36 years back on the world's biggest stage. Across three matches, he posted a 90% pass completion rate and led Canada with 186 passes completed and 50 line breaks from possession.

14

DALE MITCHELL

FORWARD / M

Born: 1958-04-21, Vancouver, BC, CAN. Height 183 cm. Dominant right foot.

1 FIFA World Cup: Group phase at Mexico 1986
1 Olympic Games: Quarterfinals at Los Angeles 1984
1 Concacaf title: 1985 Concacaf Championship
4 cycles FWC Qualifiers: 1980-81, 1985, 1988, 1992-93
1st #CANMNT: 1980-09-15 at Vancouver, BC, CAN (v. NZL)
1st Two Goals: 1980-09-15 at Vancouver, BC, CAN (v. NZL)

CANADA SOCCER HALL OF FAME

Dale Mitchell made 72 international appearances for Canada, ranked second all-time after his last Canada match on 15 August 1993 in Sydney, Australia. He retired ranked second all-time with 23 Canada goals and first all-time with 19 international "A" goals. He represented Canada at both the 1984 Olympic Games and 1986 FIFA World Cup. At the youth level, he played at the 1976 Concacaf Youth Championship.

He was Canada's top goalscorer across FIFA World Cup Qualifiers in 1985 when Canada won the Concacaf Championship. His opening goal against Guatemala on 20 April 1985 at Victoria, scored with his left foot from just outside the box, was described by coach Tony Waiters as one of the greatest goals he had ever seen.

Mitchell helped the Vancouver 86ers win three Canadian Soccer League Championships (1988 to 1990), the North American Championship (1990), and the APSL regular season title (1993).

He played his first seven seasons in the NASL with the Vancouver Whitecaps, Portland Timbers and Manic de Montréal. He scored more than 400 goals as an indoor player with the Tacoma Stars, Kansas City Comets and Baltimore Blast.

CANADA RECORDS

INT'L RECORDS	MP	MS	MIN		
1977 CANADA	0	0	0		
1980 CANADA	8	8	-	3	
1981 CANADA	7	4	405	2	
1983 CANADA	6	6	540		
1984 CANADA	7	6	596	3	
1985 CANADA	6	6	540	5	
1986 CANADA	6	5	-		
1987 CANADA	2	2	156	1	1
1988 CANADA	6	6	540	3	1
1989 CANADA	2	2	180		1
1991 CANADA	3	3	270	3	
1992 CANADA	8	8	720	3	3
1993 CANADA	11	9	831		3
17 SEASONS	**72**	**65**	**n/a**	**23**	**9**
FWC QUALIFIERS	25	22	1960	9	4
GOLD CUP	3	3	270	3	

FIFA / OLYMPIC	MP	MS	MIN	G	A
1984 OLYMPIC	4	4	390	3	
1986 FIFA WC	1	1	90		

● ● ●

1984 OLYMPIC GAMES • Dale Mitchell scored three goals in four matches at the 1984 Olympic Football Tournament. He played in every Canada minute as they reached the Quarterfinals before they were eliminated by Brazil on kicks from the penalty mark. Mitchell scored twice against Cameroon and once against Brazil.

FORWARD

14

• **DOMENIC MOBILIO**

Born: 1969-01-14, Vancouver, BC, CAN.   Height 180 cm.
Dominant left foot.   Death: 2004-11-13.

3 cycles FIFA World Cup Qualifiers: 1988, 1992-93, 1996-97
1st #CANMNT: 1986-01-29 at Vancouver, BC, CAN (v. PAR)
1st Goal: 1993-04-18 at Burnaby, BC, CAN (v. HON)

CANADA SOCCER HALL OF FAME

Domenic Mobilio made 30 career international appearances across 12 years from 1986 to 1997, including three cycles of FIFA World Cup Qualifiers and one edition of the Concacaf Gold Cup. He reached FIFA's intercontinental playoff in 1993 and the Concacaf Final Round in 1997. He also helped Canada win the 1989 Jeux de la Francophonie in Morocco.

After representing Canada at the 1985 Concacaf Under-16 Championship, he was the Men's National Team's youngest debutant in 1986 at age 17 in a 0-0 draw with Paraguay at Vancouver's BC Place.

In 1994, Mobilio featured in front a Canadian-record crowd at Edmonton's Commonwealth Stadium when Canada drew 1-1 with the soon-to-be FIFA World Cup champions Brazil.

Mobilio helped the Vancouver 86ers win four Canadian Soccer League Championships (1988 to 1991), the North American Championship (1990), and the APSL regular season title (1993). He was a three-time CSL All-Star, CSL Golden Boot winner, and two-time APSL or A-League All League Second Team forward. He was posthumously inducted to Vancouver's Ring of Honour in 2014.

Mobilio was just 18 years old when he made his professional debut with the 86ers on 7 June 1987. He played three indoor seasons with the Baltimore Blast where he won two regular season titles, but lost in the playoff final in both 1989 and 1990.

CANADA RECORDS

INT'L RECORDS	MP	MS	MIN	G	A
1986 CANADA	3	1	-		
1988 CANADA	4	3	250	3g	
1989 CANADA	4	4	360	1g	1a
1992 CANADA	2	2	101		1a
1993 CANADA	9	6	523	3g	
1994 CANADA	3	2	162		
1995 CANADA	0	0	0		
1996 CANADA	3	2	114		
1997 CANADA	2	0	90		
12 SEASONS	**30**	**20**	**n/a**	**7g**	**2a**
FWC QUALIFIERS	13	6	625	3g	
GOLD CUP	2	2	127		

• • •

FIFA WORLD CUP QUALIFIERS • Domenic Mobilio scored three goals for Canada in FIFA World Cup Qualifiers in 1993. His match winner against El Salvador in El Salvador gave Canada just their second-ever competitive away win against an opponent with 20,000 or more spectators in attendance. (25,000 fans at Estadio Cuscatlán).

4

TERRY MOORE

CENTRE BACK

Born: 1958-06-02, Moncton, NB, CAN. Grew up in Belfast, NIR. Height 183 cm. Dominant right foot.

1 FIFA World Cup: Group phase at Mexico 1986
1 Olympic Games: Quarterfinals at Los Angeles 1984
1 Concacaf title: 1985 Concacaf Championship
1 cycle FIFA World Cup Qualifiers: 1985
1st #CANMNT: 1981-10-14 at Pointe-à-Pitre, GLP (v. GLP)

 CANADA SOCCER HALL OF FAME

Terry Moore made 22 career international appearances for Canada from 1981 until 1987, including every minute of Canada's run to the Olympic Quarterfinals in 1984. He was part of the team that qualified Canada for the Olympic Games on 18 April 1984 at Royal Athletic Park in Victoria, helped Canada win the 1985 Concacaf Championship to qualify for the FIFA World Cup (although he missed the last qualification match through suspension), and was part of the squad that went to the 1986 FIFA World Cup in Mexico.

Moore was 23 years old when he made his Canada debut on 14 October 1981 in a 2-1 win over Guadeloupe at Stade Pierre-Antonius in Pointe-à-Pitre. At centre back, he was part of his first clean sheet for a 1-0 away win over Haiti at Port-au-Prince on 28 March 1984. The following year, he was part of a big 1-0 away win over Honduras in FIFA World Cup Qualifiers at Tegucigalpa.

Moore was a club legend at Glentoran FC in Northern Ireland. From 1984-85 through 1991-92, the club won two league titles, five Irish Cups and two Irish League Cups. In all, he made 333 appearances with the club.

In between his career with Glentoran FC, Moore played five seasons in the North American Soccer League with the San Diego Sockers and Tulsa Roughnecks. With Tulsa, he won the NASL Championship in 1983 and was named an NASL Second Team All-Star in 1984.

CANADA RECORDS

INT'L RECORDS	MP	MS	MIN
1981 CANADA	1	0	45
1983 CANADA	1	1	90
1984 CANADA	9	9	-
1985 CANADA	6	6	540
1986 CANADA	3	3	270
1987 CANADA	2	2	180
7 SEASONS	**22**	**21**	**n/a**
FWC QUALIFIERS	*3*	*3*	*270*

FIFA / OLYMPIC	MP	MS	MIN
1984 OLYMPIC	4	4	390
1986 FIFA WC	0	0	0

1984 OLYMPIC GAMES • Terry Moore played every Canada minute at the 1984 Olympic Football Tournament when Canada reached the Quarterfinals. In the group phase, they drew 1-1 with Iraq, lost 1-0 to Yugoslavia, and won 2-1 over Cameroon. In the Quarterfinals, they were eliminated by Brazil on kicks from the penalty mark.

WINGER / F

ISSEY NAKAJIMA-FARRAN

Born: 1984-05-16, Calgary, AB, CAN. Grew up in Tokyo, JPN & London, ENG. Height 179 cm. Dominant right foot.

3 cycles FIFA World Cup Qualifiers: 2008, 2012, 2015
1st #CANMNT: 2006-11-15 at Székesfehérvár, HUN (v. HUN)
1st Goal: 2008-06-15 at Kingstown, VIN (v. VIN)

CANADA HIGHLIGHTS

Issey Nakajima-Farran played 11 years for Canada, including three cycles of FIFA World Cup Qualifiers and three editions of the Concacaf Gold Cup. He notably helped Canada reach the Concacaf Gold Cup Semifinals in 2007.

He was 22 years old when he made his Canada debut on 15 November 2006 in a 1-0 loss to Hungary. He featured in three Concacaf Gold Cup matches the following year, including the last 10-plus minutes of the Semifinals when onside Atiba Hutchinson scored the disallowed 2-2 equaliser against the Americans. In 2008, Nakajima-Farran featured in a 3-2 loss to Copa América champions Brazil.

CLUB HIGHLIGHTS

Nakajima-Farran won league titles across his professional career in Japan, Denmark and Australia. Alongside those countries, he also played in England, Singapore, Cyprus, Canada, Malaysia and Spain, including matches in UEFA Cup and Concacaf Champions League.

In Denmark, he helped both Vejle BK and AC Horsens win promotion to the Superliga after winning Danish 1st Division titles in 2005-06 and 2009-10. In between those two clubs, he spent the bulk of his Superliga career with FC Nordsjælland.

He won the J2 League with Albirex Niigata in 2003 and the Australian A-League Championship with Brisbane Roar in 2012.

CANADA RECORDS

"A" RECORDS	MP	MS	MIN	G	A
2006 CANADA	1	0	45		
2007 CANADA	7	2	285		
2008 CANADA	8	8	613	1g	
2009 CANADA	3	1	137		
2010 CANADA	4	1	116		1a
2011 CANADA	1	0	4		
2012 CANADA	0	0	0		
2013 CANADA	6	3	261		
2014 CANADA	3	3	207		
2015 CANADA	4	3	255		
2016 CANADA	1	0	45		
11 SEASONS	**38**	**21**	**1968**	**1g**	**1a**
FWC QUALIFIERS	6	6	449	1g	
GOLD CUP	6	2	210		

1st INTERNATIONAL GOAL • Issey Nakajima-Farran scored his first international goal in 2008 FIFA World Cup Qualifiers when Canada won 3-0 away at Kingstown, St. Vincent and the Grenadines. That year, he played in a career-high eight international "A" matches for Canada. In a training match in February 2008, he scored against Vejle Boldklub.

7

MARTIN NASH

MIDFIELDER / W

Born: 1975-12-27, Regina, SK, CAN. Grew up in Victoria, BC, CAN. Height 180 cm. Dominant right foot.

1 Concacaf title: 2000 Concacaf Gold Cup
2 cycles FIFA World Cup Qualifiers: 1997, 2000
1st #CANMNT: 1997-04-06 at Burnaby, BC, CAN (v. SLV)
1st Goal: 2000-01-11 at Devonshire Parish, BER (v. BER)

CANADA HIGHLIGHTS

Martin Nash led Canada with three assists when they won the 2000 Concacaf Gold Cup, the Men's National Team's second confederation title in program history. That same season, he set a Canada record for assists in a year (five) and helped Canada set a program record with a 15-match unbeaten streak (1999-2000).

After representing Canada at the Concacaf Youth Championship and Concacaf Olympic Qualifiers, he was just 21 years old when he made his international "A" debut during the 1997 Concacaf Final Round of FIFA World Cup Qualifiers.

CLUB HIGHLIGHTS

Nash was a two-time USL A-League Championship winner with the Rochester Raging Rhinos (2000, 2001) and two-time USL First Division Championship winner with Vancouver Whitecaps FC (2006, 2008). With the Whitecaps, he was the team's MVP and Fan Favourite in 2007, named team captain in 2009, and won the team's Golden Boot award in 2010.

He played his club football in Canada, England and the United States, notably helping Stockport County win promotion from the Second Division in 1996-97. After a six-week spell as a teenager at Tottenham Hotspur FC in 1994-95, he officially made his pro debut with the Vancouver 86ers on 20 May 1995.

On 1 July 2008, he became the first Canadian to score in the newly-established Canadian Championship when he scored Vancouver's 1-0 match winner away against Toronto FC.

CANADA RECORDS

"A" RECORDS	MP	MS	MIN	G	A
1997 CANADA	8	6	467		
2000 CANADA	13	7	753	2g	5a
2001 CANADA	1	0	9		
2002 CANADA	1	1	90		1a
2003 CANADA	6	4	342		2a
2004 CANADA	1	1	55		
2006 CANADA	1	0	34		
2007 CANADA	6	5	370		1a
2008 CANADA	1	1	90		
12 SEASONS	**38**	**25**	**2210**	**2g**	**9a**
FWC QUALIFIERS	14	9	807		1a
GOLD CUP	9	7	578		3a

CONCACAF GOLD CUP • Martin Nash was a big part of Canada's run to a Concacaf title in 2000 when they won the Gold Cup at Los Angeles Memorial Coliseum with a 2-0 victory over Colombia. His corner kick in the Final was headed home by captain Jason deVos for the tournament winner.

FORWARD

OLIVIER OCCEAN

17

Born: 1981-10-23, Brossard, QC, CAN. Height 185 cm. Dominant right foot.

3 cycles FIFA World Cup Qualifiers: 2004, 2008, 2011-12
1st #CANMNT: 2004-05-30 at Wrexham, WAL (v. WAL)
1st Goal: 2005-02-09 at Belfast, NIR (v. NIR)

CANADA HIGHLIGHTS

Olivier Occean made 28 career international "A" appearances across nine years from 2004 to 2012, including three cycles of FIFA World Cup Qualifiers and one edition of the Concacaf Gold Cup. In all, he scored six international goals for Canada.

Occean made one appearance with Canada's U-23 squad before he made his international "A" debut on 30 May 2004 in an away 1-0 loss to Wales. Three months later he got his first start and made his debut in FIFA World Cup Qualifiers in a 2-0 loss to Guatemala. He scored his first international goal on 9 February 2005 when he scored the 1-0 match winner against Northern Ireland in Belfast.

CLUB HIGHLIGHTS

Occean won the 2.Bundesliga title in 2011-12 with SpVgg Greuther Fürth when he was also the league's joint top goalscorer with 17 goals. He then joined Eintracht Frankfurt where he made his Bundesliga debut in 2012-13. He scored his first Bundesliga goal less than a month later on 16 September in a 3-2 win over Hamburger SV.

Occean moved to Norway in 2004 where he played for Odd Grenland and then Lillestrøm SK (where he won the Norway Cup in 2007). Across his two stints in Norway, he scored 120 career goals across all competitions and divisions.

CANADA RECORDS

"A" RECORDS	MP	MS	MIN	G	A
2004 CANADA	7	2	260		1a
2005 CANADA	5	4	331	1g	
2006 CANADA	0	0	0		
2007 CANADA	4	1	129	1g	
2008 CANADA	1	0	9		
2010 CANADA	1	1	74		
2011 CANADA	5	3	271	3g	
2012 CANADA	5	5	369	1g	
9 SEASONS	**28**	**16**	**1443**	**6g**	**1a**
FWC QUALIFIERS	15	8	785	4g	1a
GOLD CUP	2	2	160		

● ● ●

FIFA WORLD CUP QUALIFIERS • Olivier Occean was Canada's joint top goalscorer across 2011-12 FIFA World Cup Qualifiers when he scored four goals in eight matches. He scored twice away against St. Lucia, once at home against St. Kitts and Nevis, and then the 1-0 away match winner against Cuba.

18

PAT ONSTAD

GOALKEEPER

Born: 1968-01-13, Vancouver, BC, CAN. Height 193 cm. Dominant right foot.

1 FIFA Confederations Cup: Group phase in 2001
1 Concacaf title: 2000 Concacaf Gold Cup
6 cycles FIFA World Cup Qualifiers: 1988, 1992-93, 1996-97, 2000, 2004, 2008
1st #CANMNT: 1988-02-18 at Devonshire Parish, BER (v. BER)
1st Clean Sheet: 1988-02-18 at Devonshire Parish, BER (v. BER)

 **CANADA SOCCER HALL OF FAME**

Pat Onstad was Canada's record holder with 65 goalkeeper appearances and 25 clean sheets, including 23 clean sheets at the "A" level and eight in FIFA World Cup Qualifiers. He reached FIFA's intercontinental playoff in 1993 and the Concacaf Final Round in 1997. He helped Canada win both the 1986 Concacaf Youth Championship and the 2000 Concacaf Gold Cup. He was also Canada Soccer's Player of the Year in 2003.

Onstad was 20 years old when he posted a clean sheet in his debut on 18 February 1988. He was 42 years old when he made his last appearances on 24 May 2010.

Onstad was a three-time MLS Cup winner and MLS Supporters' Shield winner with the San Jose Earthquakes and Houston Dynamo. He was a two-time MLS Goalkeeper of the Year. From 1990 to 1999, he won the CSL Championship, the CIAU Championship (three times), Canada Soccer's National Championships, the A-League regular season (three times), the A-League Championship, and the US Open Cup.

CANADA RECORDS

INT'L RECORDS	MP	MS	MIN	CS
1988 CANADA	12	12	1080	5 CS
1989 CANADA	2	2	180	1 CS
1991 CANADA	1	1	90	0 CS
1992 CANADA	1	1	90	1 CS
1993 CANADA	3	3	225	1 CS
1994 CANADA	0	0	0	0 CS
1995 CANADA	2	1	133	0 CS
1996 CANADA	0	0	0	0 CS
1997 CANADA	0	0	0	0 CS
1998 CANADA	1	1	90	1 CS
1999 CANADA	9	9	810	4 CS
2000 CANADA	10	10	900	6 CS
2001 CANADA	1	1	90	0 CS
2002 CANADA	0	0	0	0 CS
2003 CANADA	4	3	270	0 CS
2004 CANADA	8	8	720	2 CS
2007 CANADA	5	5	450	2 CS
2008 CANADA	5	5	450	2 CS
2010 CANADA	1	1	90	0 CS
23 SEASONS	**65**	**63**	**5668**	**25 CS**
FWC QUALIFIERS	*18*	*18*	*1620*	*8 CS*
GOLD CUP	*5*	*5*	*450*	*2 CS*
3 NATIONS CUP	*1*	*1*	*90*	*0 CS*

CONFEDERATIONS	MP	MS	MIN	
2001 FIFA CC	0	0	0	

PLAYER OF THE YEAR • Pat Onstad was Canada Soccer's Player of the Year in 2003 after he helped the San Jose Earthquakes lift the Rothenberg Trophy as MLS Cup champions. He was the MLS Goalkeeper of the Year and he set a Canadian record with nine clean sheets in an MLS season.

MIDFIELDER

JONATHAN OSORIO

21

Born: 1992-06-12, Brampton, ON, CAN, CAN. Height 175 cm. Dominant right foot.

1 FIFA World Cup: Group phase at Qatar 2022
1 Concacaf medal: Silver in 2022-23 CNL
1st place FIFA World Cup Qualifiers in 2021-22
1st #CANMNT: 2013-05-28 at Edmonton, AB, CAN (v. CRC)
1st Goal: 2017-01-22 at Devonshire Park, BER (v. BER)

CANADA HIGHLIGHTS

Jonathan Osorio helped Canada win the 2021-22 Concacaf Final Round of FIFA World Cup Qualifiers, participate in their first men's FIFA World Cup in 36 years, and win a Concacaf Silver Medal at the 2022-23 Nations League Finals.

Osorio was just 20 years old when he made his international "A" debut as a substitute in a 1-0 home loss to Costa Rica at Edmonton's Commonwealth Stadium. He scored his first goal in a 2017 away win over Bermuda and scored his first home goal at Toronto's BMO Field later that year against Jamaica. He has also scored international goals against Cuba (twice), US Virgin Islands, Barbados, Martinique and Honduras, but none bigger than his 1-1 away equaliser against Mexico at Estadio Azteca in FIFA World Cup Qualifiers.

TORONTO FC

Osorio won the Concacaf Champions League Golden Boot in 2018 after he led Toronto FC to the Grand Final. He is a three-time Canadian Championship winner, MLS Supporters' Shield winner and MLS Cup winner. He won the George Gross Memorial Trophy as MVP of the 2018 Canadian Championship. He has made more than 300 career appearances with the club and he was named team captain ahead of the 2024 season.

CANADA RECORDS

"A" RECORDS	MP	MS	MIN	G	A
2013 CANADA	8	4	398		
2014 CANADA	1	0	28		
2015 CANADA	4	3	208		1a
2016 CANADA	2	2	164		
2017 CANADA	4	3	257	2g	1a
2018 CANADA	3	3	270	1g	
2019 CANADA	9	7	642	1g	4a
2020 CANADA	3	3	217	1g	
2021 CANADA	15	11	931	2g	1a
2022 CANADA	11	6	617		
2023 CANADA	11	8	756	2g	1a
UNTIL DEC.2023	71	50	4488	9g	8a
FWC QUALIFIERS	17	12	928	1g	2a
GOLD CUP	19	14	1341	2g	
NATIONS LEAGUE	10	6	613	2g	5a

FIFA WORLD CUP	MP	MS	MIN
2022 FIFA WC	3	1	119

● ● ●

2022 FIFA WORLD CUP • Jonathan Osorio featured in all three Canada matches at the FIFA World Cup in Qatar. Returning from a pre-tournament injury, he featured as a substitute in the first two matches, then got the start in the group finale against Morocco. In that last match, he led Canada with a 97% pass completion rate.

13

MIDFIELDER / F

GEORGE PAKOS

Born: 1952-08-14, Victoria, BC, CAN. Height 178 cm.

1 FIFA World Cup: Group phase at Mexico 1986
1 Concacaf title: 1985 Concacaf Championship
1 cycle FIFA World Cup Qualifiers: 1985
1st #CANMNT: 1983-05-08 at Burnaby, BC, CAN (v. BER)
1st Goal: 1983-05-08 at Burnaby, BC, CAN (v. BER)

CANADA HIGHLIGHTS

George Pakos scored 10 goals in 33 career international matches across a five-year stretch with Canada. He represented Canada at the FIFA World Cup Mexico 1986 and featured in their group finale against the Soviet Union.

Pakos was 30 years old when he scored in his international debut in 1983 Olympic Qualifiers at Burnaby's Swangard Stadium in a 6-0 win over Bermuda. He scored the 1-1 away equaliser a week later in Hamilton, Bermuda. Across five years with Canada, he scored goals away against Belize, Honduras, St. Vincent and the Grenadines and the United States as well as goals at neutral venues against Uruguay in Miami, Florida and against Congo in Beijing, China.

CLUB HIGHLIGHTS

Pakos played his club football on Vancouver Island where he was the Pacific Coast League's Rookie of the Year in 1972-73, the last season before the league was renamed the BC Soccer League. He scored 12 goals as a rookie as Victoria West United finished second in the league.

With Victoria London Boxing AC (later known as the Athletics) he won Canada Soccer's 1975 National Championships. He was the Vancouver Island League's Most Valuable Player in 1974-75.

He played up until his last season in 1989 when he joined the Canadian Soccer League's expansion Victoria Vistas.

CANADA RECORDS

INT'L RECORDS	MP	MS	MIN	G	A
1983 CANADA	8	8	-	4g	
1984 CANADA	2	2	180	1g	
1985 CANADA	14	11	-	4g	1a
1986 CANADA	7	4	-	1g	
1987 CANADA	2	1	89		
5 SEASONS	**33**	**26**	**n/a**	**10g**	**1a**
FWC QUALIFIERS	*6*	*5*	*458*	*2g*	

FIFA WORLD CUP	MP	MS	MIN
1986 FIFA WC	1	0	21

FIFA WORLD CUP QUALIFIERS • George Pakos scored his two biggest goals in Canada's 1985 run to the Concacaf Championship, the 1-0 away match winner against Honduras in Tegucigalpa and then the opening goal of a 2-1 home win over Honduras at King George V Park in St. John's.

Top 100 Men's Footballers | 85

FORWARD

BUZZ PARSONS

Born: 1950-12-16, Burnaby, BC, CAN. Grew up in Vancouver, BC, CAN. Height 175 cm. Dominant right foot.

2 cycles FIFA World Cup Qualifiers: 1972, 1976-77
1st #CANMNT: 1971-05-30 at Hamilton, BER (v. BER)
1st Goal: 1971-05-30 at Hamilton, BER (v. BER)

CANADA SOCCER HALL OF FAME

Les "Buzz" Parsons made 45 career international appearances for Canada, ranked second all-time after his last Canada match on 17 September 1980 at Edmonton. Across 10 years, he represented Canada in two cycles of FIFA World Cup Qualifiers and two cycles of Olympic Qualifiers.

He scored 13 Canada goals, including a goal in his 1971 debut against Bermuda. He notably scored the match winner against Colombia in Colombia at the 1971 Pan American Games and the 1-0 match winner over Mexico at Vancouver's Empire Stadium in 1976 FIFA World Cup Qualifiers.

He also scored the opening goal of a big 3-2 win over USA at St. John's King George V Park in 1972.

Parsons was an NASL Championship winner in 1979 with the Vancouver Whitecaps, the highlight to an eight-year professional career. He was an NASL Second Team All-Star in 1977 after he scored 10 goals in 25 matches.

Parsons played his youth soccer in British Columbia before he played in the Pacific Coast League, Western Canada League, BC Premier League and BC League. He won Canada Soccer's 1971 National Championships with Eintracht SC Vancouver and the BC League twice with Vancouver Italia / Vancouver Italian Canadians Paul's.

CANADA RECORDS

INT'L RECORDS	MP	MS	MIN	G	A
1971 CANADA	12	11	-	6g	
1972 CANADA	4	4	360	1g	
1973 CANADA	8	8	631	2g	
1974 CANADA	6	5	437		
1975 CANADA	4	3	-		
1976 CANADA	3	2	254	1g	
1977 CANADA	6	5	425	3g	
1980 CANADA	2	1	-		
10 SEASONS	**45**	**39**	n/a	13g	
FWC QUALIFIERS	12	10	984	5g	
PAN AMERICAN	8	7	-	5g	

FIFA WORLD CUP QUALIFIERS • Buzz Parsons was Canada's top goalscorer across the 1976-77 FIFA World Cup Qualifiers when he scored four goals in eight international matches. He scored goals at Estadio Azteca against Suriname and Guatemala as well goals both in Vancouver and Monterrey against Mexico.

10

PAUL PESCHISOLIDO

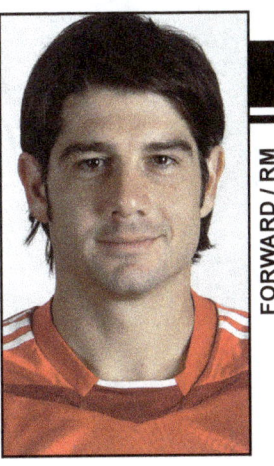

FORWARD / RM

Born: 1971-05-25, Scarborough, ON, CAN. Grew up in Pickering, ON, CAN. Height 170 cm. Dominant right foot.

1 FIFA Confederations Cup: Group phase in 2001
1 Concacaf title: 2000 Concacaf Gold Cup
4 cycles FWC Qualifiers: 1992-93, 1996-97, 2000, 2004
1st #CANMNT "A": 1992-06-13 at Toronto, ON, CAN (v. HKG)
1st Goal: 1992-06-13 at Toronto, ON, CAN (v. HKG)

CANADA SOCCER HALL OF FAME

Paul Peschisolido made 53 international "A" appearances for Canada from 1989 to 2004, helping his nation win the Concacaf Gold Cup and then feature at the FIFA Confederations Cup Korea/Japan 2001. He took part in four cycles of FIFA World Cup Qualifiers, reached the FIFA intercontinental playoff in 1993 and the Concacaf Final Round in 1997. He co-led Canada in goals in both 1995 and 1996 and he was Canada Soccer's Player of the Year in 1996.

Peschisolido was Canada's record holder with 10 international "A" goals scored in home matches, including his first Canada goal scored as a debutant at Toronto's Varsity Stadium on 13 June 1992. He scored his last international goal exactly 12 years later on 13 June 2004, the opening goal of a 4-0 home win over Belize.

Peschisolido spent 16 seasons in England from 1992-93 to 2007-08 where he scored more than 100 goals across league and cup competitions. He was Fulham FC's Player of the Season in 1997-98, then helped the squad win the Second Division and promotion in 1998-99.

Before Peschisolido moved to England, he played four seasons in the Canadian Soccer League with the Toronto Blizzard. He was a two-time CSL All-Star. He was 18 years old when he made his professional debut on 28 May 1989.

CANADA RECORDS

"A" RECORDS	MP	MS	MIN	G	A
1992 CANADA	4	2	221	1g	
1993 CANADA	7	3	318		1a
1995 CANADA	6	6	475	4g	1a
1996 CANADA	5	5	346	3g	
1997 CANADA	5	5	350		
1999 CANADA	1	1	90		1a
2000 CANADA	12	10	821	1g	
2001 CANADA	5	3	288		
2003 CANADA	3	3	216		
2004 CANADA	5	3	295	1g	
13 SEASONS	**53**	**41**	**3420**	**10g**	**3a**
FWC QUALIFIERS	26	18	1528	4g	
GOLD CUP	6	5	425		1a

CONFEDERATIONS	MP	MS	MIN
2001 FIFA CC	3	2	188

PLAYER OF THE YEAR • Paul Peschisolido was Canada Soccer's Player of the Year in 1996, the same year he transferred from Stoke City to West Bromwich Albion. He also scored three goals that year in FIFA World Cup Qualifiers. He went on to score a career-best 15 goals in 1996-97 as West Bromwich Albion finished fourth in the First Division.

MIDFIELDER

SAMUEL PIETTE

Born: 1994-11-12, Le Gardeur, QC, CAN, CAN. Height 171 cm. Dominant right foot.

1 FIFA World Cup: Group phase at Qatar 2022
1st place FIFA World Cup Qualifiers in 2021-22
1st #CANMNT: 2012-06-03 at Toronto, ON, CAN (v. USA)

CANADA HIGHLIGHTS

Samuel Piette helped Canada return to the men's FIFA World Cup for the first time in 36 years when they won the Concacaf Final Round of FIFA World Cup Qualifiers in 2022. A Men's National Team player since he was just 17 years old, Piette has already made 67 international "A" appearances across 12 years including three cycles of FIFA World Cup Qualifiers and five editions of the Concacaf Gold Cup.

At the youth level, Piette represented Canada at the FIFA U-17 World Cup Mexico 2011. With the U-23 squad, he twice helped Canada climb to within a victory of making the Olympic Games after they reached the Concacaf Semifinals in 2012 and 2015 (he was team captain in 2015).

When he made his international "A" debut in Canada's centennial match in 2012 at Toronto's BMO Field, he became the third youngest player in Men's National Team history. Since 2020, he has already made four Canada starts wearing the captain's armband.

CF MONTRÉAL

Piette helped CF Montréal win the Canadian Championship in 2019 and 2021 as well as finish third in the 2021 MLS standings. He was named the team's captain in 2023.

CANADA RECORDS

"A" RECORDS	MP	MS	MIN	G	A
2012 CANADA	1	0	4		
2013 CANADA	6	3	335		
2014 CANADA	2	0	11		
2015 CANADA	12	9	893		1a
2016 CANADA	8	3	342		
2017 CANADA	8	8	720		2a
2018 CANADA	3	3	270		
2019 CANADA	6	6	540		1a
2020 CANADA	3	3	192		
2021 CANADA	11	4	435		
2022 CANADA	6	5	322		
2023 CANADA	1	1	61		
UNTIL DEC.2023	67	45	4125		4a
FWC QUALIFIERS	17	7	1081		1a
GOLD CUP	14	11	1028		2a
NATIONS LEAGUE	4	3	294		

FIFA WORLD CUP	MP	MS	MIN
2022 FIFA WC	0	0	0

CONCACAF GOLD CUP • Samuel Piette led Canada in international minutes played in 2017, the same year Canada returned to the knockout phase at the Concacaf Gold Cup for the first time in eight years. Canada also reached the Quarterfinals in 2019, then reached the Semifinals in 2021.

TOMASZ RADZINSKI

FORWARD / LW

Born: 1973-12-14, Poznań, POL. Grew up in Jnowroclaw, POL & Toronto, ON, CAN. Height 174 cm. Dominant right foot.

3 cycles FIFA World Cup Qualifiers: 1996-97, 2004, 2008
1st #CANMNT: 1995-06-04 at Toronto, ON, CAN (v. TUR)
1st Goal: 1996-01-12 at Los Angeles, CA, USA (v. BRA)

CANADA SOCCER HALL OF FAME

Tomasz Radzinski scored 10 goals and 12 assists in 46 international "A" appearances from 1995 to 2009, including three cycles of FIFA World Cup Qualifiers and one edition of the Concacaf Gold Cup. He was Canada's all-time record holder with eight career assists in FIFA World Cup Qualifiers after leading his nation in assists during the 1996-97 cycle and co-leading Canada during the 2008 cycle. He helped Canada reach the Concacaf Final Round of 1996-97 FIFA World Cup Qualifiers. He was Canada Soccer's Player of the Year in 1998.

After representing Canada at the 1994 Jeux de la Francophonie, he made his international "A" debut on 4 June 1995 against Turkey at Toronto's Varsity Stadium. He scored his first international goal at the 1996 Concacaf Gold Cup against Brazil and recorded a pair of assists in a memorable 2-0 away win over El Salvador in FIFA World Cup Qualifiers. Twelve years later, he scored against Mexico in a 2-2 home draw at Edmonton.

Radzinski spent seven seasons in Belgium where he won two Championnats de Belgique and one Supercoupe with RSC Anderlecht as well as one Coupe de Belgique with KFC Germinal Ekeren. He was the league's top scorer in 2000-01. He then moved to England where he spent the next six seasons in the Premier League with Everton FC and Fulham FC.

CANADA RECORDS

"A" RECORDS	MP	MS	MIN	G	A
1994 CANADA	0	0	0		
1995 CANADA	4	3	264		1a
1996 CANADA	7	7	559	1g	3a
1997 CANADA	2	2	180		
1999 CANADA	0	0	0		
2001 CANADA	1	1	57		
2002 CANADA	2	2	180	2g	
2003 CANADA	3	3	270	2g	1a
2004 CANADA	7	7	568	2g	1a
2005 CANADA	2	1	135		
2006 CANADA	4	4	360	1g	
2007 CANADA	4	4	303	1g	2a
2008 CANADA	9	9	621	1g	4a
2009 CANADA	1	1	85		
16 SEASONS	**46**	**44**	**3582**	**10g**	**12a**
FWC QUALIFIERS	*19*	*19*	*1566*	*3*	*8a*
GOLD CUP	*2*	*2*	*135*	*1*	

PLAYER OF THE YEAR • Tomasz Radzinski was Canada Soccer's Player of the Year in 1998. He split that year in Belgium between KFC Germinal Ekeren (12 goals from January to May in all competitions) and RSC Anderlecht (another two goals from October to December).

MIDFIELDER

4

RANDY RAGAN

Born: 1959-06-07, High Prairie, AB, CAN. Grew up in Aldergrove, BC, CAN. Height 183 cm. Dominant right foot.

1 FIFA World Cup: Group phase at Mexico 1986
1 Olympic Games: Quarterfinals at Los Angeles 1984
1 Concacaf title: 1985 Concacaf Championship
2 cycles FIFA World Cup Qualifiers: 1985, 1988
1st #CANMNT: 1979-04-05 at Hamilton, BER (v. USA)

CANADA SOCCER HALL OF FAME

Randy Ragan made 58 international appearances for Canada, ranked third all-time after his last international match on 30 May 1987. He represented Canada at the 1984 Olympic Games, lifted the Greg Kafaty Trophy as the 1985 Concacaf Championship, and featured at the 1986 FIFA World Cup in Mexico.

After representing Canada at the 1976 Concacaf Youth Championship in Puerto Rico, he made his international debut with the Men's National Team as a teenager on 5 April 1979 in Bermuda. He made his "A" debut in a 4-0 win over New Zealand on 15 September 1980 at Vancouver. In a historic away win over Honduras in 1985, he got the assist on George Pakos' 1-0 match winner after he won an interception in the midfield.

Ragan played five years in the NASL with the Toronto Blizzard from 1980 to 1984. He was 20 years old when he made his pro debut on 5 June 1980 and he won the Blizzard's Most Valuable Player award as a sophomore in 1981. They reached the NASL final in 1983 and 1984.

After the FIFA World Cup, Ragan played for the Toronto Blizzard where he was an all-star in the league's inaugural season. After two years away completing his law degree, he played with the Victoria Vistas in 1990 and the North York Rockets in 1991.

CANADA RECORDS

INT'L RECORDS	MP	MS	MIN	G	A
1979 CANADA	2	2	180		
1980 CANADA	6	5	-		
1983 CANADA	8	8	-		
1984 CANADA	14	14	1290		
1985 CANADA	12	11	1035		2a
1986 CANADA	12	12	1080		
1987 CANADA	4	4	360		1a
9 SEASONS	58	56	n/a		
FWC QUALIFIERS	10	9	838		2a

FIFA / OLYMPIC	MP	MS	MIN
1984 OLYMPIC	4	4	390
1986 FIFA WC	3	3	270

● ● ●

1986 FIFA WORLD CUP • Randy Ragan was one of three players that featured in every Canada minute at both the 1984 Olympic Football Tournament in the United States and the 1986 FIFA World Cup in Mexico. In the 1984 Olympic Quarterfinals against Brazil, he won a dangerous free kick from which Dale Mitchell struck the crossbar.

11

TOSAINT RICKETTS

WINGER / FORWARD

Born: 1987-08-06, Edmonton, AB, CAN. Height 181 cm. Dominant right foot.

2 cycles FIFA World Cup Qualifiers: 2011-12, 2015-16
1st #CANMNT: 2011-02-09 at Larissa, GRE (v. GRE)
1st Goal: 2011-06-01 at Toronto, ON, CAN (v. ECU)

CANADA HIGHLIGHTS

Tosaint Ricketts scored 17 goals and four assists in 61 career Canada matches across 12 years. He represented Canada in two cycles of FIFA World Cup Qualifiers and four editions of the Concacaf Gold Cup. He reached the Quarterfinals at the 2017 Concacaf Gold Cup.

After he played at the FIFA U-20 World Cup Canada 2007, Ricketts helped Canada's U-23 squad climb to within a victory of qualifying for the Beijing 2008 Olympic Games. He earned his first call up to the Men's National Team in 2009, then made his international "A" debut in a narrow 1-0 away loss to Greece on 9 February 2011. He scored his first goal that year at Toronto's BMO Field in a 2-2 home draw with Ecuador.

CLUB HIGHLIGHTS

Ricketts helped Toronto FC win the MLS Supporters' Shield, Canadian Championship and MLS Cup in a trophy-filled 2017 campaign. He won another Canadian Championship in 2018.

Ricketts won the Lithuanian Supercup in 2019 with FK Sūduva Marijampolė and his third career Canadian Championship in 2022 with Vancouver Whitecaps FC. Across his career, he played in Canada, USA, Finland, Romania, Norway, Turkey Israel, and Lithuania, including appearances in UEFA and Concacaf club competitions.

In Vancouver, he was a two-time Whitecaps FC Humanitarian of the Year recipient.

CANADA RECORDS

"A" RECORDS	MP	MS	MIN	G	A
2009 CANADA	0	0	0		
2011 CANADA	9	1	221	3g	1a
2012 CANADA	9	6	619	2g	
2013 CANADA	12	8	732		
2014 CANADA	5	5	435	2g	
2015 CANADA	12	12	975	5g	1a
2016 CANADA	7	6	482	2g	2a
2017 CANADA	3	1	114	1g	
2018 CANADA	2	1	90	1g	
2020 CANADA	2	2	156	1g	
12 SEASONS	**61**	**42**	**3824**	**17g**	**4a**
FWC QUALIFIERS	20	12	1230	7g	3a
GOLD CUP	8	4	456		

FIFA WORLD CUP QUALIFIERS • Tosaint Ricketts was Canada's joint top goalscorer across 2015-16 FIFA World Cup Qualifiers when he scored four goals in nine matches. He scored all four goals at BMO Field in Toronto: two goals in a 4-0 win over Dominica in June 2015 and then another two goals in a 3-0 win over Belize in September 2015.

MIDFIELDER / CB

BRIAN ROBINSON

Born 1948-06-29, Victoria, BC, CAN. Height 173 cm.

2 cycles FIFA World Cup Qualifiers: 1972, 1976-77
1st #CANMNT: 1972-08-20 at St. John's, NL, CAN (v. USA)
1st Goal: 1972-09-05 at México, DF, MEX (v. MEX)

CANADA SOCCER HALL OF FAME

Brian Robinson made 26 career international appearances for Canada, including two cycles of FIFA World Cup Qualifiers and one cycle of Olympic Qualifiers.

In September 1972, he scored his first international goal against Mexico. Four years later playing as a sweeper, he was part of Canada's first-ever FIFA World Cup Qualifiers win over Mexico, although he was injured in that 1-0 home victory at Vancouver's Empire Stadium.

Robinson was 28 years old when he played his last international match in FIFA World Cup Qualifiers on 22 December 1976, a 3-0 win over USA at Port-au-Prince, Haiti. At the time, he ranked tied-for-seventh in all-time Canada appearances.

In his hometown Victoria, Robinson played his club football in the Pacific Coast League, Western Canada League, BC Premier League, BC League and Vancouver Island League. He won two Pacific Coast League titles with Victoria United O'Keefe. He was just 17 years old when he made his Pacific Coast League debut on 24 September 1967.

In 1975, Robinson helped Victoria London Boxing Club win Canada Soccer's National Championships. The following year, he joined the NASL's Vancouver Whitecaps where he won the club's Most Improved Player award. He missed the 1977 NASL season recovering from an injury, then joined Victoria Athletics in 1977-78.

CANADA RECORDS

INT'L RECORDS	MP	MS	MIN	G	A
1972 CANADA	3	1	134	1g	
1973 CANADA	8	8	-	2g	
1974 CANADA	7	7	599		
1975 CANADA	5	5	-		
1976 CANADA	3	3	204		
1977 CANADA	0	0	0		
6 SEASONS	**26**	**24**	**n/a**	**3g**	
FWC QUALIFIERS	*6*	*4*	*338*	*1g*	

FIFA WORLD CUP QUALIFIERS • Brian Robinson made his Canada debut in 1972 FIFA World Cup Qualifiers, a memorable 3-2 win over the Americans at King George V Park in St. John's. Sixteen days later, he became the first Canadian to score an international goal at Mexico's Estadio Azteca, a 30-yard drive into the top corner.

5

RANDY SAMUEL

CENTRE BACK / RB

Born: 1963-12-23, Point Fortin, TRI. Grew up in Saskatoon, SK & Richmond, BC, CAN. Height 185 cm. Dominant right foot.

1 FIFA World Cup: Group phase at Mexico 1986
1 Concacaf title: 1985 Concacaf Championship
4 cycles FWC Qualifiers: 1985, 1988, 1992-93, 1996-97
1st #CANMNT: 1983-12-08 at Belmopán, BLZ (v. BLZ)

 CANADA SOCCER HALL OF FAME

Randy Samuel was Canada's record holder with 88 career international appearances, including 82 "A" appearances and 36 career appearances in FIFA World Cup Qualifiers up until his last match on 16 November 1997. He helped Canada win the 1985 Concacaf Championship and he featured at the 1986 FIFA World Cup in Mexico.

After representing Canada at the 1982 Concacaf Youth Championship, he was just 19 years old when he played his first two international matches in December 1983 against Belize and Honduras. He went on to feature in four cycles of FIFA World Cup Qualifiers, most notably helping Canada beat Honduras at King George V Park to qualify for the 1986 FIFA World Cup. He also helped Canada win the 1990 Three Nations Cup after a 2-1 win over Mexico at Burnaby's Swangard Stadium.

He spent more than a decade in Europe after the 1986 FIFA World Cup playing with PSV Eindhoven, FC Volendam, Fortuna Sittard, Port Vale and Harstad IL. Before moving to Europe, he won the 1983 Canadian Pro League Championship as a rookie with the Edmonton Eagles.

CANADA RECORDS

INT'L RECORDS	MP	MS	MIN	G	A
1983 CANADA	2	2	180		
1984 CANADA	7	6	-		
1985 CANADA	16	13	1191		
1986 CANADA	9	8	765		
1988 CANADA	6	6	570		
1989 CANADA	1	1	90		
1990 CANADA	1	1	90		
1991 CANADA	2	2	180		
1992 CANADA	7	7	630		1a
1993 CANADA	11	10	952		
1994 CANADA	3	3	270		
1995 CANADA	8	8	700		
1996 CANADA	6	6	540		
1997 CANADA	9	9	810		
14 SEASONS	**88**	**82**	**n/a**		**1a**
FWC QUALIFIERS	36	34	3156		1a
GOLD CUP	5	4	382		
3 NATIONS CUP	1	1	90		

FIFA WORLD CUP	MP	MS	MIN
1986 FIFA WC	3	3	270

1986 FIFA WORLD CUP • Randy Samuel featured in every Canada minute at the 1986 FIFA World Cup in Mexico. He was lined up at centre back alongside Ian Bridge for all three matches, including Canada's impressive debut against European champions France at Estadio León (a 1-0 loss on Sunday 1 June 1986).

FORWARD

BRANKO ŠEGOTA

20

Born: 1961-06-08, Rijeka, YUG. Grew up in Toronto, ON, CAN. Height 178 cm. Dominant right foot.

1 FIFA World Cup: Group phase at Mexico 1986
2 cycles FIFA World Cup Qualifiers: 1980-81, 1988
1st #CANMNT: 1979-04-01 at Devonshire Parish, BER (v. BER)
1st Goal: 1979-04-08 at Hamilton, BER (v. MEX)

CANADA SOCCER HALL OF FAME

Branko Šegota made 28 international appearances from 1979 to 1988 including three appearances at the 1986 FIFA World Cup. He was part of the Canada squad that came within a goal of reaching the 1982 FIFA World Cup in Spain, then helped Canada qualify for the 1984 Olympic Games with a historic 0-0 draw against Costa Rica at Victoria.

Šegota led Canada in goals at both the 1978 Concacaf Youth Championship in Honduras and 1979 FIFA World Youth Championship in Japan. He was just 17 years old when he made his international debut in between those two competitions on 1 April 1979, then recorded an assist in his "A" debut on 18 October 1980 for the 1-1 draw with visiting Mexico. He scored his first competitive goal on 1 November 1980 against the United States, the match winner in a 2-1 victory at Vancouver.

Šegota was a nine-time Major Indoor League Championship winner, three times with the New York Arrows and six times with the San Diego Sockers. He was a five-time all-star from 1978-79 to 1991-92 and he was the second-highest scoring player in league history. Including playoffs, he scored more than 500 goals as an indoor player.

From 1979 to 1984, he played six seasons in the North American Soccer League with the Rochester Lancers, Fort Lauderdale Strikers and Golden Bay Earthquakes. In 1988, he played for the Toronto Blizzard.

CANADA RECORDS

INT'L RECORDS	MP	MS	MIN	G	A
1979 CANADA	3	3	270	1g	1a
1980 CANADA	3	2	225	1g	1a
1981 CANADA	9	9	-	3g	1a
1984 CANADA	3	1	-		1a
1985 CANADA	1	1	60		
1986 CANADA	4	0	92		
1987 CANADA	3	2	-		
1988 CANADA	2	1	80		
10 SEASONS	**28**	**19**	**n/a**	**5g**	
FWC QUALIFIERS	8	8	695	1g	2a

FIFA WORLD CUP	MP	MS	MIN		
1986 FIFA WC	3	0	72		

1986 FIFA WORLD CUP • Branko Šegota featured in all three Canada matches at the FIFA World Cup in Mexico. Nursing an injury through the MISL playoffs in May, he missed part of Canada's preparation camp and was limited to a role off the bench during Canada's first participation on the world's biggest stage.

11

JOSH SIMPSON

LEFT WINGER

Born: 1983-05-15, Burnaby, BC, CAN. Grew up in Victoria, BC, CAN. Height 183 cm. Dominant left foot.

2 cycles FIFA World Cup Qualifiers: 2008, 2011-12
1st #CANMNT: 2004-01-18 at Bridgetown, BRB (v. BRB)
1st Goal: 2010-09-07 at Montréal, QC, CAN (v. HON)

CANADA HIGHLIGHTS

Josh Simpson represented Canada in two cycles of FIFA World Cup Qualifiers and three editions of the Concacaf Gold Cup. He led Canada in minutes played in 2011, but then missed the next round of FIFA World Cup Qualifiers after suffering a career-ending leg injury in Switzerland. He was just 28 years old when he played his last international match on 29 February 2012 in Cyprus against Armenia.

Five weeks after helping Canada U-20 reach the Quarterfinals at the 2003 FIFA World Youth Championship, Simpson made his international "A" debut on 18 January 2004 against Barbados.

CLUB HIGHLIGHTS

Simpson played eight seasons in Europe before he suffered a broken leg on 23 May 2012, the last day of the 2011-12 season with third-place BSC Young Boys. He had spent just half a season in Switzerland after playing in England, Germany and Turkey, including two matches in the UEFA Cup in 2004.

Simpson had his best offensive season in 2010-11 when he led Manisaspor with 12 goals (also ranked seventh-best in the Turkish Süper Lig). The previous season, he helped Manisapor reach the Semifinals in the Turkish Cup.

In retirement, he was honoured by The Soccer Hall of Fame of British Columbia in 2022.

CANADA RECORDS

"A" RECORDS	MP	MS	MIN	G	A
2004 CANADA	6	2	229		
2005 CANADA	7	4	442		1a
2006 CANADA	2	2	180		
2007 CANADA	2	1	81		
2008 CANADA	1	0	17		
2009 CANADA	8	5	490		2a
2010 CANADA	4	3	293	1g	1a
2011 CANADA	12	11	937	3g	2a
2012 CANADA	1	1	61		
9 SEASONS	**43**	**29**	**2730**	**4g**	**6a**
FWC QUALIFIERS	11	7	653	3g	1a
GOLD CUP	10	8	711		2a

1st INTERNATIONAL GOAL • Josh Simpson scored his first international "A" goal and earned Player of the Match honours in a 2-1 home win over Honduras at Montréal's Stade Saputo on 7 September 2010. The following year, he scored international goals against St. Lucia (two) and St. Kitts and Nevis during FIFA World Cup Qualifiers.

RIGHT BACK / M

PAUL STALTERI

Born: 1977-10-18, Etobicoke, ON, CAN. Grew up in Brampton, ON, CAN. Height 180 cm. Dominant right foot.

1 FIFA Confederations Cup: Group phase in 2001
1 Concacaf title: 2000 Concacaf Gold Cup
3 cycles FIFA World Cup Qualifiers: 2000, 2004, 2008
1st #CANMNT: 1997-08-17 at Toronto, ON, CAN (v. IRN)
1st Goal: 1999-06-02 at Edmonton, AB, CAN (v. GUA)

CANADA SOCCER HALL OF FAME

Paul Stalteri was Canada's record holder with 84 career international "A" appearances from 1996 to 2011. He was a Concacaf Gold Cup champion in 2000 and Canada Soccer Player of the Year in both 2001 and 2004. He also made 30 Canada starts wearing the captain's armband. He was a Concacaf Gold Cup all-star in 2007 when Canada reached the Semifinals.

Stalteri featured at the 1993 FIFA U-17 World Cup in Japan, won the 1996 Concacaf Youth Championship in Mexico, and reached the knockout phase at the 1997 FIFA World Youth Championship in Malaysia. He scored in his international debut on 14 July 1996 against Portugal's amateur team at Toronto, but then made his proper "A" debut a year later against Iran in Toronto.

Stalteri was a double winner in 2003-04 with SV Werder Bremen when he won both the Bundesliga and DFB-Pokal. He spent five seasons with the club and reached the last 16 in UEFA Champions League in 2004-05. In England, he played for Tottenham Hotspur FC and Fulham FC in the Premier League. He then returned to Germany where he played two seasons with Borussia Mönchengladbach.

CANADA RECORDS

"A" RECORDS	MP	MS	MIN	G	A
1996 CANADA	0	0	0		
1997 CANADA	1	0	45		
1998 CANADA	1	1	90		
1999 CANADA	10	10	876	1g	1a
2000 CANADA	15	15	1324		2a
2001 CANADA	5	5	450	1g	
2002 CANADA	7	7	680	1g	2a
2003 CANADA	8	8	720	3g	
2004 CANADA	2	2	180		
2005 CANADA	1	1	90		
2006 CANADA	2	2	180		
2007 CANADA	10	10	889	1g	1a
2008 CANADA	11	11	939		
2009 CANADA	6	6	517		
2010 CANADA	5	5	450		
2011 CANADA	0	0	0		
16 SEASONS	**84**	**83**	**7430**	**7g**	**6a**
FWC QUALIFIERS	16	16	1415		
GOLD CUP	20	20	1862	1g	3a

CONFEDERATIONS	MP	MS	MIN
2001 FIFA CC	3	3	270

● ● ●

PLAYER OF THE YEAR • Paul Stalteri was a two-time Canada Soccer Player of the Year in a four-year span when he played for SV Werder Bremen in Germany. In 2001, he played in every Canada minute at the FIFA Confederations Cup, including a 0-0 draw with Brazil. He scored later that year in an away friendly loss to Malta in November 2001.

13

KENNY STAMATOPOULOS

GOALKEEPER

Born: 1979-08-28, Kalamata, GRE. Grew up in Markham, ON, CAN. Height 188 cm. Dominant left foot.

2 cycles FIFA World Cup Qualifiers: 2011-12, 2015-16
1st #CANMNT: 2001-11-14 at Paola, MLT (v. MLT)
1st Clean Sheet: 2005-11-16 at Hesperange, LUX (v. LUX)

CANADA HIGHLIGHTS

Goalkeeper Kenny Stamatopoulos has made 21 Canada appearances and posted nine clean sheets. He has represented Canada in two cycles of FIFA World Cup Qualifiers and two editions of the Concacaf Gold Cup.

Four months after representing Canada at the 2001 Jeux de la Francophonie, Stamatopoulos made his international "A" debut on 14 November 2001 against Malta. Nearly four years later, he made his next international appearance in a 2-1 loss to Spain on 3 September 2005. Another two months later, he posted his first clean sheet in a 1-0 win over Luxembourg.

AIK FOTBOLL

Stamatopoulos joined AIK Fotboll in Stockholm in 2010 after which he has spent more than a decade with the club. He made a career-high 26 appearances in 2013 when the club finished runners up in the Allsvenskan. He was also part of the squad that won the Johanssons Trophy as league champions in 2018.

Before Stamatopoulos joined AIK Fotboll, he played in Canada, Greece, Sweden and Norway.

Through 2024, Stamatopoulos is still active as a goalkeeper (and goalkeeper coach) with AIK Fotboll.

CANADA RECORDS

"A" RECORDS	MP	MS	MIN	CS
2001 CANADA	1	0	45	0 CS
2002 CANADA	0	0	0	0 CS
2003 CANADA	0	0	0	0 CS
2004 CANADA	0	0	0	0 CS
2005 CANADA	2	2	180	1 CS
2006 CANADA	2	2	180	1 CS
2007 CANADA	0	0	0	0 CS
2008 CANADA	0	0	0	0 CS
2009 CANADA	0	0	0	0 CS
2011 CANADA	2	2	180	2 CS
2012 CANADA	1	0	45	0 CS
2013 CANADA	2	2	135	1 CS
2014 CANADA	0	0	0	0 CS
2015 CANADA	9	8	728	4 CS
2016 CANADA	2	1	139	0 CS
16 SEASONS	**21**	**17**	**1632**	**9 CS**
FWC QUALIFIERS	*6*	*6*	*416*	*4 CS*
GOLD CUP	*3*	*3*	*270*	*2 CS*

CONCACAF GOLD CUP • Kenny Stamatopoulos was named Canada's Most Valuable Player at the 2015 Concacaf Gold Cup. He posted two clean sheets and conceded just one goal in a loss to Jamaica, but it was not enough to advance Canada out of the group phase that year.

FORWARD / W

• MIKE STOJANOVIĆ

7

Born 1947-01-26, Lapovo, YUG. Height 185 cm. Dominant right foot. Death 2010-11-18.

1 cycle FIFA World Cup Qualifiers: 1980-81
1st #CANMNT: 1980-09-15 at Vancouver, BC, CAN (v. NZL)
1st Goal: 1980-09-15 at Vancouver, BC, CAN (v. NZL)

CANADA SOCCER HALL OF FAME

Momčilo "Mike" Stojanović was Canada's top goalscorer across FIFA World Cup Qualifiers in 1980 and 1981. Across two years with Canada Soccer's Men's National Team, he scored seven goals in 18 international matches, including three goals in those FIFA World Cup Qualifiers when Canada came within a goal of qualifying for the 1982 FIFA World Cup in Spain.

He was 33 years old when he scored in his international debut in a 4-0 home win over New Zealand at Vancouver's Empire Stadium. Just 33 days later, Stojanović scored his first FIFA World Cup Qualifiers goal in a 1-1 home draw with Mexico at Toronto's Exhibition Stadium.

He made his last international appearance on 21 November 1981, a 2-2 draw with Cuba that eliminated Canada from FIFA World Cup Qualifiers. He was already out of professional football when Canada qualified for the 1984 Olympic Games and 1986 FIFA World Cup.

Stojanović played for FK Radnički in Yugoslavia's First Division before he moved to Toronto where he joined the Toronto Serbian White Eagles. He won the National League Ontario title in 1974 and was the league's top goalscorer that same season.

Stojanović played seven seasons in the North American Soccer League with the Rochester Lancers, San Diego Sockers and San Jose Earthquakes. He was 29 years old when he made his NASL debut on 23 April 1976.

He was an NASL Second Team All-Star in 1977 and the NASL North American Player of the Year in 1982. He set a San Diego club record with 23 goals scored in 1981.

CANADA RECORDS

INT'L RECORDS	MP	MS	MIN	G	A
1980 CANADA	9	8	-	4g	1a
1981 CANADA	9	9	-	3g	
2 SEASONS	**18**	**17**	**n/a**	**7g**	
FWC QUALIFIERS	9	9	805	3g	

FIFA WORLD CUP QUALIFIERS • Mike Stojanović featured in all five Canada matches in the 1981 Concacaf Final Round of FIFA World Cup Qualifiers in Honduras. He scored the 1-0 match winner against El Salvador on the opening day and the 1-1 equaliser against Haiti in Canada's second match.

15

ADAM STRAITH

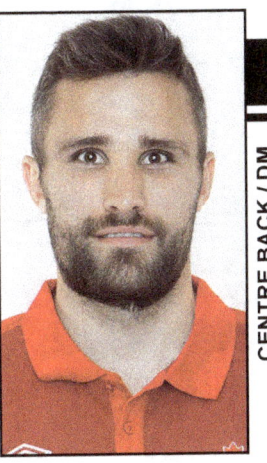

CENTRE BACK / DM

Born: 1990-09-11, Surrey, BC, CAN. Grew up in Victoria, BC, CAN. Height 189 cm. Dominant right foot.

2 cycles FIFA World Cup Qualifiers: 2011-12, 2015-16
1st #CANMNT: 2010-05-24 at Buenos Aires, ARG (v. ARG)

CANADA HIGHLIGHTS

Adam Straith made 43 international "A" appearances across 10 years from 2010 to 2019, including two cycles of FIFA World Cup Qualifiers and three editions of the Concacaf Gold Cup.

Straith was just 19 years old when he made his international "A" debut as a substitute in an away loss to Argentina shortly before the 2010 FIFA World Cup. He got his first start five days later in a 1-1 away draw with Venezuela and put forth a Player of the Match performance later that year in a 2-0 home loss to Peru.

Across his career, he earned Player of Match honours four times, including a 4-2 away win in Bermuda when he played most of the second half as the emergency goalkeeper after an injury to second-half substitute Sean Melvin.

CLUB HIGHLIGHTS

Straith played his club football in Canada, Germany and Norway, including parts of three seasons in the 2.Bundesliga with FC Energie Cottbus. He was 19 years old when he made his 2.Bundesliga debut on 25 October 2009.

Straith grew up playing his youth soccer in British Columbia and played for the Vancouver Whitecaps Residency program before he moved overseas to Germany. In 2017, he played for FC Edmonton in the North American Soccer League.

CANADA RECORDS

"A" RECORDS	MP	MS	MIN	G	A
2010 CANADA	5	4	369		
2011 CANADA	5	5	450		2a
2012 CANADA	1	1	61		
2013 CANADA	4	4	356		
2014 CANADA	5	4	377		
2015 CANADA	12	12	1058		1a
2016 CANADA	8	7	630		
2017 CANADA	3	2	195		
2019 CANADA	0	0	0		
10 SEASONS	**43**	**39**	**3496**		**3a**
FWC QUALIFIERS	13	12	1106		2a
GOLD CUP	3	3	270		

FIFA WORLD CUP QUALIFIERS • Adam Straith represented Canada in back-to-back cycles of FIFA World Cup Qualifiers. He played in nine matches during the 2015-16 campaign and earned Player of the Man honours in a 0-0 away draw with El Salvador at Estadio Cuscatlán.

GREG SUTTON

GOALKEEPER

Born: 1977-04-19, Hamilton, ON, CAN. Grew up in Bethel, CT, USA. Height 198 cm. Dominant right foot.

2 cycles FIFA World Cup Qualifiers: 2004, 2008
1st #CANMNT: 2004-01-18 at Bridgetown, BRB (v. BRB)
1st Clean Sheet: 2004-01-18 at Bridgetown, BRB (v. BRB)

CANADA HIGHLIGHTS

Greg Sutton represented Canada in two cycles of FIFA World Cup Qualifiers and three editions of the Concacaf Gold Cup. He made 16 international "A" appearances and posted seven clean sheets.

From back-to-back Concacaf Gold Cups, he helped Canada reach the 2007 Semifinals and 2009 Quarterfinals, although he was limited to just the one group stage match in 2007 before he suffered a concussion and missed the rest of the tournament.

Sutton was 26 years old when he posted a clean sheet in his international "A" debut against Barbados on 18 January 2004.

CLUB HIGHLIGHTS

Sutton was a four-time USL A-League / First Division Goalkeeper of the Year and the 2004 USL A-League Most Valuable Player during a six-year stint with the Montréal Impact. He won the USL A-League Championship in 2004 and then the Commissioner's Cup as regular-season winners in both 2005 and 2006.

Sutton had a brief second stint with the Impact in 2011 and 2012 and he was honoured on the club's Wall of Fame in 2019.

Sutton grew up playing his youth soccer in Connecticut before he made his MLS debut on 19 June 1999 with the Chicago Fire. In between his two stints with Montréal, he played with expansion Toronto FC and then New York Red Bulls.

Before turning pro, he played his college football at St. Lawrence University.

CANADA RECORDS

"A" RECORDS		MP	MS	MIN	CS	
1999	CANADA	0	0	0	0	CS
2004	CANADA	1	1	90	1	CS
2005	CANADA	5	5	450	1	CS
2006	CANADA	2	2	180	2	CS
2007	CANADA	2	2	180	0	CS
2008	CANADA	1	1	90	0	CS
2009	CANADA	5	4	405	3	CS
11 SEASONS		**16**	**15**	**1395**	**7**	**CS**
FWC QUALIFIERS		0	0	0	0	CS
GOLD CUP		8	8	720	2	CS

CONCACAF GOLD CUP • Goalkeeper Greg Sutton featured in every Canada minute at the 2009 Concacaf Gold Cup when they reached the Quarterfinals. In the group phase, he posted back-to-back clean sheets against Jamaica and El Salvador before Canada won the group with a 2-2 draw against Costa Rica.

11

MIKE SWEENEY

MIDFIELDER / FB

Born: 1959-12-25, Duncan, BC, CAN. Grew up in Squamish, BC, CAN. Height 170 cm. Dominant left foot.

1 FIFA World Cup: Group phase at Mexico 1986
1 Olympic Games: Quarterfinals at Los Angeles 1984
1 Concacaf title: 1985 Concacaf Championship
4 cycles FWC Qualifiers: 1980-81, 1985, 1988, 1992-93
1st #CANMNT: 1979-04-01 at Devonshire Parish, BER (v. BER)
1st Goal: 1979-05-27 at Ottawa, ON, CAN (v. BER)

 CANADA SOCCER HALL OF FAME

Mike Sweeney was Canada's record holder with 81 career appearances, including 61 international "A" appearances up until his last match on 15 August 1993 in Australia. Across his 15-year international career, he helped Canada reach the Quarterfinals at the 1984 Olympic Games, win the 1985 Concacaf Championship (although he missed the match in St. John's through suspension), and feature at the FIFA World Cup for the first time ever at Mexico 1986.

Sweeney was just 19 years old when he made his international debut on 1 April 1979 in Bermuda. He scored his first goal eight weeks later in the return match against Bermuda in Ottawa. On 17 September 1980, Sweeney made his "A" debut in a 3-0 win over New Zealand at Edmonton's Commonwealth Stadium. He scored his first FIFA World Cup Qualifiers goal on 13 April 1985 in a big 2-0 home win over Haiti at Victoria's Royal Athletic Park.

Sweeney played five seasons in the North American Soccer League with the Edmonton Drillers, Vancouver Whitecaps and Golden Bay Earthquakes.

After the NASL, he played seven seasons in the MISL with the indoor Cleveland Force, Minnesota Strikers, Baltimore Blast and Cleveland Crunch. He also played one season in the Canadian Soccer League.

CANADA RECORDS

INT'L RECORDS	MP	MS	MIN	G	A
1979 CANADA	4	4	360	1g	
1980 CANADA	8	5	-		
1981 CANADA	8	7	541		
1983 CANADA	6	6	540		
1984 CANADA	9	9	840	2g	
1985 CANADA	7	7	598	1g	1a
1986 CANADA	10	9	773		
1988 CANADA	9	9	777		1a
1990 CANADA	2	2	180		
1992 CANADA	8	8	664		1a
1993 CANADA	10	10	885		2a
15 SEASONS	**81**	**76**	**n/a**	**4g**	
FWC QUALIFIERS	*29*	*25*	*2294*	*1g*	*4a*
3 NATIONS CUP	*2*	*2*	*180*		

FIFA / OLYMPIC	MP	MS	MIN
1984 OLYMPIC	4	4	390
1986 FIFA WC	2	1	98

1984 OLYMPIC GAMES • Mike Sweeney featured in every Canada minute at the 1984 Olympic Football Tournament in the United States, including the 1-1 draw with Brazil in the Quarterfinals when Canada were eliminated on kicks from the penalty mark. He scored two goals in an Olympic Qualifiers match that year against Cuba.

WINGER / MIDFIELDER

CARL VALENTINE

7

Born: 1958-07-04, Manchester, ENG.   Height 175 cm. Dominant right foot.

1 FIFA World Cup: Group phase at Mexico 1986
1 Concacaf title: 1985 Concacaf Championship
3 cycles FIFA World Cup Qualifiers: 1985, 1988, 1992-93
1st #CANMNT: 1985-09-14 at St. John's, NL, CAN (v. HON)
1st Goal: 1992-06-13 at Toronto, ON, CAN (v. HKG)

CANADA SOCCER HALL OF FAME

Carl Valentine delivered the corner kicks that led to both Canada goals in their big 2-1 win over Honduras on 14 September 1985 at King George V Park, the day that Canada qualified for the FIFA World Cup for the first time in program history. After his impressive international debut, he made another 30 "A" appearances for Canada from 1986 to 1993, including every Canada minute of the 1986 FIFA World Cup in Mexico.

He represented Canada in two more cycles of FIFA World Cup Qualifiers, including a trip to FIFA's intercontinental playoffs in 1993. He also represented Canada at the first Concacaf Gold Cup in 1991. He scored his first and only goal for Canada on 13 June 1992, the match winner at Toronto's Varsity Stadium in a 3-1 win over Hong Kong.

Valentine played in England with Oldham Athletic before he moved to Canada where he won the 1979 NASL Championship with the Vancouver Whitecaps. He played six seasons in the NASL before the league folded, then moved back to England where he played parts of two seasons in the First Division with West Bromwich Albion.

Valentine played seven seasons in the MISL with the indoor Cleveland Force, Baltimore Blast, Kansas City Comets and Tacoma Stars. In the summers, he played for the Vancouver 86ers in the Canadian Soccer League, APSL and A-League. He won four-straight CPL Championships from 1988 to 1991.

CANADA RECORDS

"A" RECORDS	MP	MS	MIN	G	A
1985 CANADA	1	1	89		
1986 CANADA	5	5	426		
1988 CANADA	3	3	270		2a
1991 CANADA	2	2	180		
1992 CANADA	10	7	668	1g	1a
1993 CANADA	10	5	580		
9 SEASONS	**31**	**23**	**2213**	**1g**	**3a**
FWC QUALIFIERS	15	9	962		1a
GOLD CUP	2	2	180		

FIFA WORLD CUP	MP	MS	MIN
1986 FIFA WC	3	3	270

1986 FIFA WORLD CUP • Carl Valentine played every Canada minute at the 1986 FIFA World Cup in Mexico when they faced France, Hungary and the Soviet Union in the group phase. He had made his international debut just nine months earlier in FIFA World Cup Qualifiers at King George V Park in St. John's.

5

STEVEN VITÓRIA

CENTRE BACK

Born: 1987-01-11, Toronto, ON, CAN. Grew up in Sudbury & Mississauga, ON, CAN. Height 195 cm. Dominant right foot.

1 FIFA World Cup: Group phase at Qatar 2022
1 Concacaf medal: Silver in 2022-23 CNL
1st place FIFA World Cup Qualifiers in 2021-22
1st #CANMNT: 2016-02-05 at Carson, CA, USA (v. USA)
1st Goal: 2016-10-06 at Marrakech, MAR (v. MTN)

CANADA HIGHLIGHTS

Steven Vitória helped Canada finish in first place in the 2021-22 Concacaf Final Round of FIFA World Cup Qualifiers and then win a Concacaf Silver Medal at the Concacaf Nations League Finals in 2023. He has made 46 career international "A" appearances, featured in two cycles of FIFA World Cup Qualifiers, and played at three Concacaf Gold Cups.

He has made six Canada starts wearing the captain's armband and he featured in all three Canada matches at the 2022 FIFA World Cup.

Vitória was 29 years old when he made his Canada debut on 5 February 2016 in a narrow 1-0 loss to the United States. Before the end of his first year with the National Team, he scored his first Canada goal on 6 October in a 4-0 win over Mauritania. Since that first year, he has also scored goals against the Americans in 2019, Curaçao and Japan in 2022, and most recently from the penalty spot against the Americans in the 2023 Concacaf Gold Cup Quarterfinals.

GD CHAVES

Vitória won Portuguese Segunda Liga titles to help both SC Olhanense (2008-09) and GD Estoril Praia (2011-12) win promotion to the top division. After he joined Benfica, he helped the club win the Primeira Liga and reach the UEFA Europa League Final. In Poland, he won the 2019 Polish Cup with Lechia Gdańsk.

CANADA RECORDS

"A" RECORDS	MP	MS	MIN	G	A
2016 CANADA	5	3	391	1g	
2017 CANADA	5	5	416		
2019 CANADA	4	3	292	1g	
2020 CANADA	0	0	0		
2021 CANADA	14	13	1223		
2022 CANADA	10	10	858	2g	
2023 CANADA	8	6	634	1g	
UNTIL DEC.2023	46	40	3814	5g	
FWC QUALIFIERS	12	11	1043		
GOLD CUP	11	10	976	1g	
NATIONS LEAGUE	10	8	740	2g	

FIFA WORLD CUP	MP	MS	MIN
2022 FIFA WC	3	3	270

2022 FIFA WORLD CUP • Centre back Steven Vitória featured in every Canada minute at the FIFA World Cup in Qatar, Canada's first participation on the world's biggest stage in 36 years. Across three group matches, he led Canada with 23 possession regains in defensive actions.

Top 100 Men's Footballers | 103

CENTRE BACK

MARK WATSON

3

Born: 1970-09-08, West Vancouver, BC, CAN. Height 185 cm. Dominant right foot.

1 FIFA Confederations Cup: Group phase in 2001
4 cycles FWC Qualifiers: 1992-93, 1996-97, 2000, 2004
1st #CANMNT: 1991-03-16 at Torrance, CA, USA (v. USA)
1st Goal: 1993-07-31 at Edmonton, AB, CAN (v. AUS)

CANADA SOCCER HALL OF FAME

Mark Watson made 78 international appearances for Canada, ranked third all-time after his last match on 13 October 2004 in his fourth cycle of FIFA World Cup Qualifiers. He helped Canada reach FIFA's intercontinental playoff in 1993, the Concacaf Final Round of FIFA World Cup Qualifiers in 1997, lift the Concacaf Gold Cup in 2000, and feature at the FIFA Confederations Cup in 2001. He led Canada in minutes played four times and won Player of the Year honours in 1997.

He was just 20 years old when he made his international debut at the 1991 North American Cup against the United States. He scored his first Canada goal two years later in the first leg of the FIFA intercontinental playoffs against Australia, scoring from a rebound shortly after a Dale Mitchell corner kick at Edmonton.

At the 2000 Concacaf Gold Cup, he scored the 1-0 match winner against Trinidad and Tobago in the Semifinals to qualify Canada for the 2001 FIFA Confederations Cup.

Watson was an all-star in the Canadian League as well as the APSL / A-League. He won the 2003 A-League regular season and playoff championships with Charleston Battery. He won two CIAU Championships at the University of British Columbia.

CANADA RECORDS

"A" RECORDS	MP	MS	MIN	G	A
1991 CANADA	4	3	353		
1992 CANADA	2	1	113		
1993 CANADA	14	14	1290	1g	
1994 CANADA	3	3	270		
1995 CANADA	9	9	761		
1996 CANADA	6	6	540	1g	
1997 CANADA	11	11	887		
1999 CANADA	5	5	405		
2000 CANADA	10	10	878	1g	
2001 CANADA	5	5	420		
2003 CANADA	1	1	90		
2004 CANADA	8	8	720		
2005 CANADA	0	0	0		
15 SEASONS	**78**	**76**	**6727**	**3g**	
FWC QUALIFIERS	34	34	2963	2g	
GOLD CUP	11	10	985	1g	
3 NATIONS CUP	1	1	90		

CONFEDERATIONS	MP	MS	MIN
2001 FIFA CC	2	2	159

● ● ●

2001 FIFA CONFEDERATIONS CUP • Mark Watson represented Canada at the 2001 FIFA Confederations Cup in Japan where he made two appearances in the group phase. As part of a three-player backline, he featured in the 3-0 opening loss to Japan as well as the 0-0 draw with Brazil.

3

BRUCE WILSON

LEFT BACK

Born: 1951-06-20, Vancouver, BC, CAN. Height 183 cm. Dominant left foot.

1 FIFA World Cup: Group phase at Mexico 1986
1 Olympic Games: Quarterfinals at Los Angeles 1984
1 Concacaf title: 1985 Concacaf Championship
1st #CANMNT: 1974-04-12 at Hamilton, BER (v. BER)

CANADA SOCCER HALL OF FAME

Bruce Wilson was Canada's captain at both the 1984 Olympic Games and 1986 FIFA World Cup, the pinnacle to a 16-year international career in which he made a record 72 Canada appearances from 1971 to 1986. He captained Canada to the 1985 Concacaf Championship when the nation qualified for the FIFA World Cup. Well after his career, he was named to Concacaf's Team of the Century.

Wilson, one of the original inductees to the Canada Soccer Hall of Fame in 2000, was Canada's leader in minutes played four times (1976, 1981, 1983, 1985) across his career. He featured in every Canada minute at the 1984 Olympic Games.

Wilson was a 1980 NASL Championship winner with the New York Cosmos. Across 11 seasons from 1974 to 1984, he was a five-time First or Second Team All-Star while playing with the Vancouver Whitecaps, Chicago Sting, Cosmos and Toronto Blizzard. He was the Whitecaps' Best Defensive Player in 1976.

Before he turned pro, Wilson played in the Western Canada League, Pacific Coast League and BC League. He was just 18 years old when he made his big league debut on 23 May 1970 with the Vancouver Spartans. He won the Pacific Coast League with Vancouver Columbus FC in 1970-71 and the BC League with Vancouver Italia FC in 1973-74.

CANADA RECORDS

INT'L RECORDS		MP	MS	MIN	G	A
1971	CANADA	0	0	0		
1974	CANADA	7	7	591		
1975	CANADA	0	0	0		
1976	CANADA	5	5	450		1a
1977	CANADA	5	5	450		
1981	CANADA	9	9	-		
1983	CANADA	7	7	630		
1984	CANADA	13	13	1200		
1985	CANADA	17	17	-		1a
1986	CANADA	9	9	761		
13 SEASONS		**72**	**72**	**n/a**		
FWC QUALIFIERS		2	2	1980		1a

FIFA / OLYMPIC		MP	MS	MIN
1984	OLYMPIC	4	4	390
1986	FIFA WC	3	3	221

1984 OLYMPIC GAMES • Captain Bruce Wilson featured in every Canada minute at the Olympic Football Tournament when Canada reached the 1984 Quarterfinals before they were eliminated by Brazil on kicks from the penalty mark. Wilson scored on Canada's first kick in the shootout, but they lost 4-2 after four rounds of kicks.

MIDFIELDER

DAVID WOTHERSPOON

Born: 1990-01-16, Perth, SCO. Grew up in Bridge of Earn, SCO. Height 172 cm. Dominant right foot.

1 FIFA World Cup: Group phase at Qatar 2022
1 Concacaf medal: Silver in 2022-23 CNL
1st place FIFA World Cup Qualifiers in 2021-22
1st #CANMNT: 2018-03-24 at San Pedro del Pinatar, ESP (v. NZL)
1st Goal: 2021-03-29 at Bradenton, FL, USA (v. CAY)

CANADA HIGHLIGHTS

David Wotherspoon has already made 13 international "A" appearances, helped Canada win the 2021-22 Concacaf Final Round of FIFA World Cup Qualifiers, and won a Concacaf Silver Medal at the 2022-23 Nations League Finals. He also helped Canada reach the Quarterfinals at the 2023 Concacaf Gold Cup.

Wotherspoon was 28 years old when he made his debut for Canada on 24 March 2018, a 1-0 win over New Zealand in San Pedro del Pinatar, Spain. He made his FIFA World Cup Qualifiers debut three years later in a 5-1 win over Bermuda and scored his first international goal four days later in an 11-0 win over Cayman Islands, the same day he tied a Canada record with three assists in a single match.

DUNDEE UNITED FC

Wotherspoon was a double winner with St. Johnstone FC in 2020-21, capturing the Scottish League Cup in February and the Scottish Cup in May. He earned Player of the Match honours in the 2021 Scottish Cup Final after he set up Shaun Rooney for the 1-0 match winner.

Across 10 seasons with St. Johnstone FC, Wotherspoon made more than 350 appearances, also winning the Scottish Cup in 2014. Before joining St. Johnstone FC in 2013-14, he made his debut in the Premiership with Hibernian FC.

Wotherspoon split the 2023-24 season between Inverness Caledonian Thistle FC and Dundee United FC.

CANADA RECORDS

"A" RECORDS	MP	MS	MIN	G	A
2018 CANADA	1	0	45		
2019 CANADA	1	1	52		
2021 CANADA	8	3	305	1g	3a
2022 CANADA	1	0	14		
2023 CANADA	2	0	72		
UNTIL DEC.2023	13	4	488	1g	3a
FWC QUALIFIERS	8	5	305	1g	3a
GOLD CUP	2	0	72		
NATIONS LEAGUE	1	1	52		

FIFA WORLD CUP	MP	MS	MIN		
2022 FIFA WC	1	0	14		

2022 FIFA WORLD CUP • David Wotherspoon represented Canada at the 2022 FIFA World Cup in Qatar after he made his way back from a lengthy recovery from injury. He featured in the last group match against Morocco, coming in as Canada's last substitute at Al Thumama Stadium.

FRANK YALLOP

RIGHT BACK / CB

Born: 1964-04-04, Watford, ENG. Grew up in New Westminster, BC, CAN. Height 180 cm. Dominant right foot.

2 cycles FIFA World Cup Qualifiers: 1992-93, 1996-97
1st #CANMNT: 1990-05-06 at Burnaby, BC, CAN (v. USA)

CANADA SOCCER HALL OF FAME

Frank Yallop made 52 international "A" appearances from 1990 to 1997, notably winning the 1990 Three Nations Cup and representing Canada in the first edition of the Concacaf Gold Cup as well as two cycles of FIFA World Cup Qualifiers.

Yallop was part of the Canada squad that reached the 1993 intercontinental playoff before they were eliminated by Australia on the road to the FIFA World Cup USA 1994. A year later, he was the lone Canadian to play every minute of their 1994 international season, including the 1-1 draw with soon-to-be FIFA World Cup champions Brazil in front of a record Canadian crowd at Edmonton's Commonwealth Stadium.

At the club level, Yallop played 12 seasons with Ipswich Town FC, including the first three seasons of the Premier League. He was just 19 years old when he made his debut with the first team on 17 March 1984. He helped Ipswich Town FC win the Second Division title in 1991-92 to earn promotion to the new Premier League.

In retirement, he was honoured by the Ipswich Town FC Hall of Fame in 2022.

In Major League Soccer, Yallop played with the Tampa Bay Mutiny and won the first MLS Supporters' Shield in 1996. He also played in the MLS All-Star Game in 1997. He led all Canadians in MLS minutes for three consecutive seasons before his retirement.

CANADA RECORDS

"A" RECORDS	MP	MS	MIN	G	A
1990 CANADA	1	1	90		
1991 CANADA	3	2	243		
1992 CANADA	9	9	782		2a
1993 CANADA	11	11	1020		
1994 CANADA	5	5	450		
1995 CANADA	6	6	540		
1996 CANADA	8	8	646		
1997 CANADA	9	9	810		
8 SEASONS	**52**	**51**	**4581**		**2a**
FWC QUALIFIERS	28	28	2476		2a
GOLD CUP	7	6	603		
3 NATIONS CUP	2	2	180		

THREE NATIONS CUP • Frank Yallop was 26 years old when he made his international debut at the 1990 North American Championship in Burnaby, British Columbia. He featured in every Canada minute across the round-robin competition, both the 1-0 win over USA and the 2-1 win over Mexico at Swangard Stadium.

FORWARD

• FRANK AMBLER

Born 1920-01-29, Avoch, SCO. Grew up in Vancouver, BC, CAN. Height 180 cm. Death 1978-03-21.

Frank Ambler was a two-time Dominion of Canada Football Championship winner as well as a five-time Pacific Coast League winner from 1940 to 1956. He was the Pacific Coast League's top goalscorer in 1946-47 and the league's third-highest goalscorer across the 1940s.

GOALKEEPER

• DICK ARENDS

Born 1916-11-17, Wijhe, Overijissel, NED. Grew up in Toronto, ON, CAN. Height 181 cm. Death: 2012-05-05.

Dick Arends won the 1946 USSFA National Challenge Trophy with the Chicago Vikings. He won multiple league titles in Toronto including the Walker Cup as 1951 National League Ontario section winners. He also won the Ontario Cup in both 1936 and 1948.

FULLBACK / IF

• EDDIE BAK

Born 1935-08-30, Edmonton, AB, CAN. Grew up in Vancouver, BC, CAN. Height 175 cm. Death: 1968-11-03.

Eddie Bak was a five-time Canada Soccer Football Championship winner and five-time Pacific Coast League winner from 1956 until his death in 1968. He also helped Firefighters win the Pacific Coast International Championship for the Kennedy Trophy in 1962 and 1966.

FORWARD / IF

• JIM BLUNDELL

Born 1939-07-29, Vancouver, BC, CAN. Height 175 cm. Dominant right foot. Death: 2019-03-31.

Jim Blundell was a Canada Soccer Football Championship winner, five-time Pacific Coast League winner, and Pacific Coast International Championship winner. He won two Pacific Coast League scoring titles and was the league's second-highest goalscorer in the 1960s.

• ROY CAIRNS

Born: 1925-02-15, Clayburn, BC, CAN. Height 168 cm.
Death 2010-11-13. He was 32 years old when he made his #CANMNT debut in FIFA World Cup Qualifiers on 22 June 1957.

Roy "Buster" Cairns was the first-ever five-time winner of the Canada Soccer Football Championship. From 1948 to 1961, he was also a four-time Pacific Coast League winner. He represented Canada in 1957 in FIFA World Cup Qualifiers.

• MARCEL CASTONGUAY

Born: 1919, Montréal, QC, CAN. Death 1969-09-15.

Marcel Castonguay was a Dominion of Canada Football Championship winner in 1948 after he scored the series-winning goal. He won the National League Championship for the Atholstan Trophy twice, the Coupe du Québec provincial title twice, and multiple league titles.

• PAUL-ÉMILE CASTONGUAY

Born 1917-11-04, Montréal, QC, CAN. Death 1975-01-18.

Paul-Émile Castonguay won the Dominion of Canada Football Championship, the Coupe du Québec and the National League Championship for the Atholstan Trophy in 1948 with Montréal Carsteel FC. In all, he won the Coupe du Québec four times.

• ROLAND CASTONGUAY

Born 1913-01-15, Montréal, QC, CAN. Height 157 cm.
Death: 1989-04-28.

Roland "Dempsey" Castonguay was the hero of the 1934 Dominion of Canada Football Championship when Verdun Park FC lifted the national title. *The Canadian Press* recognised him in 1950 as one of the top Canadian footballers from the first half century.

1940s - 1970s Top Footballers | 109

LEFT BACK

• JACK COWAN

Born: 1927-06-06, Vancouver, BC, CAN. Height 184 cm. Death 2000-12-10. He was 29 years old when he represented Canada in 1956.

Jack Cowan won back-to-back Scottish League Cups in 1951 and 1952 before he won the Canada Soccer Football Championship in 1956. *The Canadian Press* recognised him in 1950 as one of the top Canadian footballers from the first half century.

OUTSIDE WING

• ERROL CROSSAN

Born 1930-10-06, Montréal, QC, CAN. Grew up in Douglas, Isle of Man. Height 170 cm. Death 2016-04-23.

Errol Crossan was a two-time Canada Soccer Football Championship winner, a Pacific Coast League winner and an Eastern Canada Pro League winner. He was an all-star in BC on either side of his career in England where he became a club legend at Norwich City FC.

HALF BACK

NEIL ELLETT

Born 1944-01-05, Vancouver, BC, CAN. Grew up in Burnaby, BC, CAN. He was 23 years old when he made his #CANMNT debut in Olympic Qualifiers on 24 June 1967.

Neil Ellett won the Canada Soccer Football Championship and Pacific Coast League playoff title before he played in the NASL with Vancouver Whitecaps FC. From 1967 to 1973, he made 20 career international appearances, at the time ranked third most with Canada.

GOALKEEPER

• BILL GILL

Born 1919-04-15, Montréal, QC, CAN. Height 183 cm. Death 1984-06-15. Represented Canada's eastern all-stars in 1947.

Bill Gill won the 1952 Canada Soccer Football Championship after an MVP performance with Montréal Stelco FC. He won multiple league titles in Montréal as well as the Coupe du Québec provincial title and National League Championship for the Atholstan Trophy.

PETER GRECO

Born 1946-07-19, Priverno, ITA. Grew up in Montréal, QC, CAN. Height 189 cm. Dominant right foot. He was 21 years old when he made his #CANMNT debut at the 1967 Pan American Games.

Peter Greco was a three-time Canada Soccer National Championship winner. MVP of the 1966 Québec National League season, he represented Canada at two Pan American Games as well as Olympic Qualifiers and FIFA World Cup Qualifiers.

• DOUG GREIG

Born: 1928-03-16, Vancouver, BC, CAN. Height 180 cm. Death 2003-03-09. He was 29 years old when he made his #CANMNT debut in FIFA World Cup Qualifiers on 22 June 1957.

Doug Greig was a five-time Pacific Coast League winner from 1946 to 1964. He also won international club tournaments in both 1953 and 1962. He represented Canada in back-to-back international opportunities in 1956 and 1957.

• TREVOR HARVEY

Born 1916-09-07, North Vancouver, BC, CAN. Death: 1988-07-24.

Trevor Harvey was a four-time Dominion of Canada Football Championship winner. He also won multiple league, Mainland Cup and BC Province Cup titles. *The Canadian Press* recognised him in 1950 as one of the top Canadian footballers from the first half century.

BOB HAZELDINE

Born 1939-02-28, Vancouver, BC, CAN. Height 180 cm.

Bob Hazeldine was a Canada Soccer Football Championship winner, a two-time Pacific Coast League winner, a Western Canada League winner, and a Pacific Coast International Championship winner from 1957 to 1972. He was a six-time all-star in a nine-year span.

HALF BACK

• WES HENDERSON

Born 1919-09-17, Vancouver, BC, CAN. Height 185 cm. Dominant right foot. Death 2002-01-30.

Wes Henderson won the 1947 Canada Soccer Football Championship with Vancouver St. Andrews FC after he earned Man of the Match honours in the second win over Winnipeg Scottish. He was a six-time Pacific Coast League winner from 1938 to 1953.

GOALKEEPER

DICK HOWARD

Born 1943-06-10, Bromborough, ENG. Height 188 cm. He was 29 years old when he made his #CANMNT debut in FIFA World Cup Qualifiers on 20 August 1972.

Dick Howard played club football in England before he moved to Canada and won the 1967 National League Ontario title with Primo FC Hamilton. He continued his pro career in the NASL and was Canada's goalkeeper for FIFA World Cup Qualifiers in 1972.

FORWARD

• ART HUGHES

Born: 1930-10-01, Camrose, AB, CAN. Grew up in Camrose & Vancouver. Death 2019-03-04. Ht 183 cm. Left foot. He was 23 years old when he made his #CANMNT debut in FWCQ on 22 June 1957.

Art Hughes was a two-time Canada Soccer Football Championship winner and seven-time Pacific Coast League winner from 1950 to 1967. He broke the league's all-time goalscoring record in his last year. He represented Canada in 1957 and 1960.

INSIDE RIGHT

• GORDON ION

Born: 1934-08-26, Vancouver, BC, CAN. Height 175 cm. Death 2019-09-21. He was 22 years old when he made his #CANMNT debut in FIFA World Cup Qualifiers on 22 June 1957.

Gordon Ion won a Pacific Coast League title in 1961-62 and he was an annual all-star selection for five consecutive seasons in the mid 1950s. He was a big league player from 1951 to 1963. He represented Canada in FIFA World Cup Qualifiers in 1957.

• BOB KELLY

Born 1932-08-04, Belfast, NIR. Height 178 cm. Death 2010-10-08.

Bob Kelly was both a National League Ontario winner and Eastern Canada Pro League winner. He was a seven-time all-star in a seven-year stretch. He was selected to play for Canada in 1960, but was not released for the four-week overseas tour.

• JOHNNY KERR

Born 1943-10-15, Glasgow, SCO. Height 168 cm. Death: 2011-06-19. He was 24 years old when he made his #CANMNT debut in FIFA World Cup Qualifiers on 6 October 1968.

Johnny Kerr won the 1967 National League Ontario title with Primo Hamilton FC and the 1972 NASL Championship with the New York Cosmos. He made 10 international appearances for Canada across two cycles of FIFA World Cup Qualifiers.

• DON MATHESON

Born 1920-05-31, Vancouver, BC, CAN. Height 180 cm. Death 1999-12-01.

Don Matheson was a Dominion of Canada Football Championship winner and six-time Pacific Coast League winner from 1938 to 1954. He was a nine-time all-star in an 11-year stretch. A two-sport all-star, he won the Mann Cup as a national lacrosse champion.

• NEIL McEACHNIE

Born 1932-04-26. Grew up in Vancouver, BC, CAN. Height 183 cm. Death 2012-01-20. He was 28 years old when he represented Canada in 1960.

Neil McEachnie was a two-time Pacific Coast League winner and two-time Pacific Coast League top scorer. He was the league's fourth-best goalscorer in the 1950s and fifth-best goalscorer in the 1960s. He played for Canada on their 1960 tour to the Soviet Union.

IL / OL

NORMIE McLEOD

Born: 1938-98-19, Vancouver, BC, CAN. Height 168 cm. Dominant left foot. He was 18 years old when he made his #CANMNT debut in FIFA World Cup Qualifiers on 22 June 1957.

Normie McLeod was a Canada Soccer Football Championship winner and two-time Pacific Coast League winner from 1955 to 1972. He was the league's third best goalscorer across the 1960s. He represented Canada in back-to-back international opportunities in 1957 and 1960.

FORWARD

• DOUG McMAHON

Born 1917-10-16, Winnipeg, MB, CAN. Height 175 cm. Death: 1997-04-16. Represented Canada's eastern all-stars in 1947 and 1949.

Doug McMahon won the 1948 Dominion of Canada Football Championship in the same year he was named Montréal's Sportsman of the Year. *The Canadian Press* recognised him in 1950 as one of the top Canadian footballers from the first half century.

CENTRE HALF

BOB MILLS

Born Vancouver, BC, CAN. Height 180 cm.

Bob Mills was a Canada Soccer Football Championship winner as well as a three-time Pacific Coast League winner. He also won the Pacific Coast International Championship twice for the Kennedy Trophy. He was a five-time all-star in a seven-year span from 1959 to 1965.

GOALKEEPER

• BOBBY NEWBOLD

Born 1919-02-04, Vancouver, BC, CAN. Height 183 cm. Death: 1995-10-11. Dominant right foot.

Bobby Newbold was a Dominion of Canada Football Championship winner and five-time Pacific Coast League winner from 1939 to 1954. He led or co-led the Pacific Coast League in clean sheets nine times and retired as the league's all-time leader.

• KEN PEARS

Born: 1934-04-12, Vancouver, BC, CAN. Height 180 cm.
Death 2022-12-18. He was 23 years old when he made his #CANMNT debut in FIFA World Cup Qualifiers on 22 June 1957.

Ken Pears won four Canada Soccer Football Championships and seven Pacific Coast League titles from 1951 to 1969. He was the league's all-time leader in clean sheets and he represented Canada in three successive opportunities (1956, 1957, 1960).

• BRIAN PHILLEY

Born: 1926-08-15, Saskatoon, SK, CAN. Grew up in Vancouver, BC. Ht 178 cm. Death 2002-08-30. He was 30 years old when he made his #CANMNT debut in FIFA World Cup Qualifiers on 22 June 1957.

Brian Philley was a two-time Canada Soccer Football Championship winner and five-time Pacific Coast League winner from 1943 to 1963. He was the league's joint second-best goalscorer in the 1950s. He represented Canada in 1956 and 1957.

• PAT PHILLEY

Born: 1929-04-24, Vancouver, BC, CAN. Height 183 cm.
Death 2019-11-22. He was 28 years old when he made his #CANMNT debut in FIFA World Cup Qualifiers on 22 June 1957.

Pat Philley was a Canada Soccer Football Championship winner and two-time Pacific Coast League winner from 1948 to 1958. He represented Canada in 1956 and 1957 and wore the captain's armband for FIFA World Cup Qualifiers in 1957.

• HARRY PHILLIPS

Born 1912-12-02, Methil, Fife, SCO. Grew up in Toronto, ON, CAN. Height 178 cm. Death: 1989-05-14. He was 34 years old when he captained Canada's eastern all-stars in 1947.

Harry Phillips was both a Dominion of Canada Football Championship winner and USSFA National Challenge Trophy winner across his career from 1933 to 1951. *The Canadian Press* recognised him in 1950 as one of the top Canadian footballers from the first half century.

GOALKEEPER

BARRY SADLER

Born: 1941-12-28, Calgary, AB, CAN. Grew up in Victoria, BC, CAN. Height 185 cm. Dominant right foot. He was 26 years old when he represented Canada in 1968.

Barry Sadler was a three-time Pacific Coast League winner and two-time Pacific Coast International Championship winner for the Kennedy Trophy. He retired as the Pacific Coast League's all-time leader in clean sheets. He was picked to play for Canada in 1968 and 1971.

FORWARD

JOHNNY SCHEPERS

Born: 1943-02-27, Tiel, NED. Grew up in Winnipeg, MB, CAN. Height 175 cm. Dominant right foot. He was 17 years old when he represented Canada in 1960.

Johnny Schepers was a Canada Soccer Football Championship winner and three-time Western Canada League winner. The WCSL's all-time leading goalscorer, he was Canada's second-best goalscorer in 1971 across Olympic Qualifiers and Pan American Games.

OUTSIDE LEFT

BOBBY SMITH

Born 1940-11-30, Vancouver, BC, CAN. Height 183.

Bobby Smith was a two-time Pacific Coast League winner and two-time Pacific Coast International Championship winner. He was a three-time Pacific Coast League scoring champion and broke the league's all-time goalscoring record in 1972.

INSIDE LEFT

• JIMMY SPENCER

Born 1915-02-13, North Vancouver, BC, CAN. Height 178 cm. Dominant left foot. Death: 1990-04-14.

Jimmy Spencer won the Dominion of Canada Football Championship on either side of World War II. He also won he Pacific Coast League, the Mainland Cup, and the BC Province Cup multiple times. He was the Pacific Coast League's top goalscorer across the 1940s.

• OSTAP STECKIW

Born 1924-03-13, Lwow, POL. Death: 2001-04-13. He was 33 years old when he scored in his #CANMNT debut in FIFA World Cup Qualifiers on 6 July 1967.

Ostap Steckiw won the 1950-51 France Division 2 league title with Olympique Lyonnais and the 1957 Canada Soccer Football Championship with SA Ukraina Montréal. He scored in his lone international match for Canada, a 3-2 win over USA in St. Louis.

JACK STEELE

Born: 1932-11-01, Victoria, BC, CAN. Grew up in Vancouver, BC, CAN. Height 173 cm. He was 24 years old when he made his #CANMNT debut in FIFA World Cup Qualifiers on 22 June 1957.

Jack Steele was a Canada Soccer Football Championship winner and three-time Pacific Coast League winner from 1950 to 1965. He was selected to represent Canada in three successive international opportunities from 1956 to 1960.

GARY STEVENS

Born 1942-01-25, Vancouver, BC, CAN. Grew up in Burnaby, BC, CAN. Height 175 cm.

Gary Stevens was a two-time Canada Soccer National Championships winner and a four-time Pacific Coast League winner from 1959 to 1975. He also helped the Firefighters win the Pacific Coast International Championship in 1962 and 1966 (he was MVP in 1966).

• GOGIE STEWART

Born: 1929-01-02, Vancouver, BC, CAN. Height 170 cm.
Death 2003-05-12. He was 28 years old when he made his #CANMNT debut in FIFA World Cup Qualifiers on 22 June 1957.

Gordon "Gogie" Stewart was a three-time Canada Soccer Football Championship winner and six-time Pacific Coast League winner from 1947 to 1965. He was selected to represent Canada in three successive international opportunities from 1956 to 1960.

RIGHT BACK

DAVID STOTHARD

Born: 1937-06-27, Vancouver, BC, CAN. Height 168 cm. Dominant right foot. He was 19 years old when he made his #CANMNT debut in FIFA World Cup Qualifiers on 22 June 1957.

David Stothard was a two-time Canada Soccer Football Championship winner and six-time Pacific Coast League winner from 1955 to 1972. He was a 10-time all-star in an 11-year span. He represented Canada in back-to-back international opportunities in 1957 and 1960.

MIDFIELDER

JENO STRENICER

Born 1945-08-12, Budapest, HUN. Height 168. Dominant right foot. He was 32 years old when he made his #CANMNT debut in FIFA World Cup Qualifiers on 8 October 1977.

Jeno Strenicer was a North American Soccer League Championship winner with Toronto Metros-Croatia in 1976. He made 11 international appearances for Canada, but missed the 1981 Concacaf Final Round of FIFA World Cup Qualifiers after he suffered an injury.

CENTRE HALF

• JOHNNY SYME

Born 1924-10-05, Glasgow, SCO. Height 188 cm. Death: 1984-08-11. Represented Canada's eastern all-stars in 1949.

Johnny Syme was a two-time National League Ontario winner with the East End Canadians after he moved to Toronto in 1949. He was an all-star selection in eight consecutive seasons from 1949 to 1956 and MVP of the National League Ontario-Québec in 1954.

CENTRE HALF

GENE VAZZOLER

Born 1941-09-25, Torino, ITA. Grew up in Burnaby, BC, CAN. Height 180 cm. Dominant right foot.

Gene Vazzoler was a four-time Canada Soccer National Championships winner as well as a multiple-time league winner in the Pacific Coast League, BC Premier League and BC League. His jersey number 5 was retired by Vancouver Columbus FC.

• JACKIE WHENT

Born 1920-05-03, Darlington, ENG. Grew up in Vancouver, BC, CAN. Height 180 cm. Death: 1999-08-25.

Jackie Whent was a Canada Soccer Football Championship winner after stints in England and USA. He also won a Pacific Coast League title. *The Canadian Press* recognised him in 1950 as one of the top Canadian footballers from the first half century.

• FRED WHITTAKER

Born 1923-04-18, Vancouver, BC, CAN. Height 183 cm. Death 2006-09-29.

Fred Whittaker won the 1949 Dominion of Canada Football Championship after he was the tournament's top goalscorer. He led the Pacific Coast League in goalscoring six times and was the second-highest goalscorer across both the 1940s and 1950s.

LES WILSON

Born 1946-07-10, Withenshawe, ENG. Grew up in Vancouver, BC, CAN. Height 175 cm.

Les Wilson won the Ed Bayley Trophy as BC Soccer's top junior player before he played his professional football in England. In 1967, he helped Wolverhampton win the United Soccer Association title when the club spent the summer as the Los Angeles Wolves.

SERGIO ZANATTA

Born 1946-08-08, ITA. Grew up in Vancouver, BC, CAN. Height 173 cm. Dominant left foot. He was 20 years old when he made his #CANMNT debut in Olympics Qualifiers on 21 June 1967.

Sergio Zanatta was a four-time Canada Soccer National Championships winner, three-time Pacific Coast League winner, and Western Canada League winner. He made 15 international appearances from 1967 to 1971, at the time ranked third most all time with Canada.

BOOKS BY UP NORTH PRODUCTIONS

Canada from Bronze to Gold
(Women's National Team 2010-2021)

Canadian Soccer's All-Time
Top 100 Women's Footballers

Canadian Soccer's 2024 Men's
Football Annual

SOCCER FOOTBALL BOOKS :

CANADA FROM BRONZE TO GOLD
CHRISTINE SINCLAIR THE G.O.A.T. - 12 FAMOUS MATCHES FOR CANADA
CANADIAN SOCCER'S ALL-TIME TOP 100 WOMEN'S FOOTBALLERS
CANADIAN SOCCER'S ALL-TIME TOP 100 MEN'S FOOTBALLERS
CANADIAN SOCCER'S 2024 MEN'S FOOTBALL ANNUAL
THIS DAY IN CANADIAN SOCCER HISTORY
CANADIAN SOCCER HISTORY: MEN'S AMATEUR FOOTBALL CHAMPIONS
26 REMARKABLE MOMENTS IN CANADIAN SOCCER HISTORY

HOCKEY BOOKS :

THE WAYNE GRETZKY GOALS RECORD
12 SEASONS: THE CWHL RECORDS BOOK
WHO'S WHO IN WOMEN'S HOCKEY GUIDE
GAME 7 : RECORDS, HEROES & CHAMPIONS

COLLECTOR BOOKS :

THE O-PEE-CHEE HOCKEY CARD STORY
1979-80 O-PEE-CHEE HOCKEY CARD STORY
THE PARKIES HOCKEY CARD STORY
THE O-PEE-CHEE MASTER CHECKLIST
THE O-PEE-CHEE HOCKEY CARD MASTER CHECKLIST
100 HOCKEY CARD FIRSTS
COLLECTING THE TOP 100: MONTRÉAL CANADIENS
COLLECTING THE TOP 100: TORONTO MAPLE LEAFS
COLLECTING THE TOP 100: O-PEE-CHEE HOCKEY CARDS
THE WAYNE GRETZKY COLLECTOR'S HANDBOOK
THE EXPOS BASEBALL CARD MASTER CHECKLIST

www.ingramcontent.com/pod-product-compliance
Lightning Source LLC
Chambersburg PA
CBHW072211070526
44585CB00015B/1296